THE TRUTH BEHIND THE DaVINCI CODE

RICHARD ABANES

HARVEST HOUSE PUBLISHERS

EUGENE, OREGON

All Scripture quotations are taken from the New American Standard Bible®, © 1960, 1962, 1963, 1968, 1971, 1972, 1973, 1975, 1977, 1995 by The Lockman Foundation. Used by permission. (www.Lockman.org)

Cover by Terry Dugan Design, Minneapolis, Minnesota

Cover and interior images (pp. 72, 73, and 74) of Leonardo da Vinci's *The Last Supper* courtesy of Santa Maria della Grazie, Milan, Italy / Bridgeman Art Library

---

Other Books by Richard Abanes

*Fantasy and Your Family: The Lord of the Rings,
Harry Potter, and Magick in the Modern World*

*Harry Potter and the Bible:
The Menace Behind the Magick*

*One Nation Under Gods:
A History of the Mormon Church*

THE TRUTH BEHIND THE DA VINCI CODE
Copyright © 2004 by Richard Abanes
Published by Harvest House Publishers
Eugene, Oregon 97402
www.harvesthousepublishers.com

Library of Congress Cataloging-in-Publication Data
Abanes, Richard.
    The truth behind the da Vinci code / Richard Abanes.
        p.   cm.
    Includes bibliographical references.
    ISBN 0-7369-1439-0 (pbk.)
    1. Brown, Dan, 1964–   Da Vinci code. 2. Mary Magdalene, Saint—In literature.
    3. Christian saints in literature. 4. Jesus Christ—In literature. 5. Christianity in lit-
    erature. I. Title.
    PS3552.R685434D33 2004
    813'.54—dc22
                                                                        2004005047

Printed in the United States of America

04   05   06   07   08   09   10 / VP-CF / 10   9   8   7   6   5   4   3   2   1

CONTENTS

Thrilled by a Thriller

John Grisham teaches you about torts. Tom Clancy teaches
you about military technology. Dan Brown gives you
a crash course in art history and the Catholic Church.

Stephen Rubin, president and publisher, Doubleday/Broadway Publishing Group[1]

Treachery, religious fanaticism, murder, an ancient conspiracy, secret societies, erotic spirituality, feminism, and inspiring legends. These are the plot elements that in 2003 helped popularize one of the most intriguing, yet disturbing, books to ever hit bestseller lists—*The Da Vinci Code* (Doubleday Publishing). This thriller by Dan Brown—a former English teacher at Phillips Exeter Academy, New Hampshire—continues to entertain millions of fiction fans. And more importantly, the novel has created a phenomenon. It is raising many thought-provoking questions in the minds of countless readers—questions directly related to some very important subjects:

- the reliability and historicity of the Bible
- the true nature of Jesus Christ
- the origin and development of Christian beliefs
- the activities of church leaders during the Christian church's formative years

How widespread is this phenomenon? Very. Several Internet sites, for example, have been devoted to discussing spiritual matters using *The Da Vinci Code* as a starting point. Churches across America are holding group discussions for those who wish to dialogue about the "facts" revealed in the book. ABC went so far as to air a TV special about Jesus Christ based on it.[2] And Hollywood will be making *The Da Vinci Code* into a movie (to be released by Sony Pictures).

"Even if you lived under a rock—a rock in a remote area of the Arizona desert—you could not avoid hearing about *The Da Vinci Code*," noted a January 2004 article.[3] This remark coincided with Brown's novel reaching its forty-fifth week as a *New York Times* bestseller, having sold nearly six million copies. Less than a year earlier, a salon.com story had predicted, "Sometime in the next few weeks, someone you know is going to tell you they've read this fantastic new thriller called *The Da Vinci Code,* and before you can stop them they will have launched into a breathless description of the plot."[4]

Dan Brown's plot, of course, is central to all of the attention the book has garnered. It is a controversial saga wrapped around what one reviewer bluntly described as "the gleefully heretical notion that the entirety of Judeo–Christian culture is founded on a misogynist [woman-hating] lie, evincing disgust for sex in general and the female body in particular."[5] But that's just the beginning point of the novel's bold accusations against just about everyone who has ever had anything to do with the rise of mainstream Christianity.

Breaking the Code

According to *The Da Vinci Code,* true Christianity was started by a Jesus Christ whom others viewed as just another prophet. He made no claims of divinity. Moreover, he was married, and his wife was none other than the well-known Mary Magdalene. She was supposedly handpicked by Christ to lead his church. After the crucifixion, however, Mary was forced to flee Jerusalem for fear of the apostle Peter, who was incensed that Jesus had chosen Mary to assume leadership of his devoted followers.[6]

Virtually everyone knew this "truth" during the earliest years of Christianity, says Brown's book. But then, by recasting Mary "as a whore in order to erase evidence of her powerful family ties," male church leaders were able to begin "the greatest cover-up in human history."[7] Although Mary survived, she did so only through the loyalty and support of Jewish protectors, with whom she found refuge in France. It was there she gave birth to Jesus' daughter. Sadly, these two outcast women had no choice but to remain in hiding for the rest of their lives, thus avoiding certain death at the hands of those who had gained control of the increasingly patriarchal church. These religious villains also changed the originally pagan, goddess-worshiping church into a Jesus-worshiping, power-crazed den of evildoers who perverted Christ's teachings to further their own political agenda.[8]

In *The Da Vinci Code* we also learn that Mary Magdalene's story would have been lost forever had it not been for her protectors. They chronicled her life, and even catalogued her descendants.[9] Brown explains, "Christ's line grew quietly under cover in France until making a bold move in the fifth century, when it intermarried with French royal blood and created a lineage known as the Merovingian bloodline."[10]

Nevertheless, the Church relentlessly sought the annihilation of all evidence relating to Mary's identity and "her family's rightful claim to power."[11] By the fifth century, of course, Mary had been long dead. But this did not stop Roman Catholic authorities from attempting to do the next best thing to killing her directly: destroying the records that told "the true story of her life."[12] These documents, secretly stashed beneath the ruins of Herod's temple in Jerusalem, were buried not only along with other important documents (for example, texts written by Christ himself), but also with Magdalene's bones themselves. Searching for this treasure was "part of what the Crusades were about. Gathering and destroying information."[13]

Church officials, however, failed in their diabolical quest because a group of truth-honoring knights stepped into the conflict. This order of warriors—known collectively as the Knights Templar—was created by a brotherhood called the Priory of Sion, a secret group allegedly founded in 1099 by the French king Godfrey of Bouillon (*Godefroi de Bouillon,* in French). He was a descendant of Jesus and Mary, according to *The Da Vinci Code,* and formed the Priory so the truth would be protected and passed on "from generation to generation."[14]

The Plot Thickens

In Jerusalem, as the story goes, the Knights recovered the precious documents. This in turn bought them considerable bargaining ability with the Vatican, which for some mysterious reason granted the Knights "limitless power."[15] Subsequently, the Knights flourished for two centuries, gaining converts, land, followers, and great wealth. But the uneasy arrangement lasted only until October of 1307, when Pope Clement V conspired with King Philip IV of France to have all the Knights rounded up and killed.

Clement's plan was executed with frightening speed and precision. Only a few Knights escaped the bloody plot. But with them remained the explosive documents that the Pope had so desperately wanted. Instead of falling into his hands, they were entrusted to the only ones still loyal to the truth—members of the Priory of Sion.

Over the years the Priory faithfully guarded their sacred treasure, allowing knowledge of it to be passed on only through codes and symbols, the most famous symbol being the Holy Grail. According to Brown, the Grail is *not* the cup Jesus used during the Last Supper. It is a metaphor for Magdalene, bearer of Christ's bloodline. And the search for the Holy Grail is an allegory for "the quest to kneel before the bones of Magdalene."[16]

Details about the Grail's location have remained sketchy—for understandable reasons—except to the Priory. Its ongoing mission has been to not only watch over the Grail and shield its location, but also to "nurture and protect the bloodline of Christ—those few members of the royal Merovingian bloodline who have survived into modern times."[17]

Exactly who are the members of the Priory of Sion? This is where Leonardo da Vinci comes into the picture. He and Sir Isaac Newton, along with the Italian painter Botticelli, the French author Victor Hugo, and many other historical figures, were all supposedly Grand Masters of the Priory. For proof of Leonardo's involvement, Brown says that one need only look at some of the artist's most famous paintings: for instance, the Mona Lisa, *The Last Supper,* and *Virgin of the Rocks.* These classic masterpieces allegedly contain numerous symbols and codes that clearly reflect Leonardo's own worship of the sacred feminine (or the goddess), his disdain for traditional Christianity, and the truth about Mary Magdalene.

Following the "Facts"

It is an understatement to say that many people have been outraged by the claims in *The Da Vinci Code*. Beyond being a page-turning thriller, Brown's novel seems to be little more than a well-crafted, cleverly written 454-page diatribe against Christianity, especially its Roman Catholic sector. The book launches repeated attacks against Christian beliefs, the Bible, and early church leaders. And when it comes to the most sacred of all Christian doctrines—those relating to Jesus—Brown writes that "almost everything our fathers taught us about Christ is *false*."[18]

Spreading one's views via fiction is certainly a freedom guaranteed to all Americans. Most critics would acknowledge that Brown has the right to say whatever he wants to say. What is problematic, however, is the way that he, his publisher, and the media have been presenting *The Da Vinci Code:* as a fact-based exposé wherein the characters reveal *truths* long hidden from, or at the very least ignored by, the general public. To use the author's words, "When you finish the book—like it or not—you've learned a ton."[19]

Nearly every reviewer has parroted this line. *USA Today*, for instance, referred to the novel as "historic fact with a contemporary storyline."[20] Popmatters.com said the work was a "fact-based thriller."[21] *Counterculture* called the book "a good yarn within a richly factual context."[22] And Charles Taylor of salon.com described the novel as "a fast-paced romp through 2000 years of Christianity's darker secrets." Taylor then added, "The most amazing thing about this novel is that it's based on fact."[23]

Only Dan Brown himself has made more explicit claims of factuality for his book. The novel's first page, for instance, reads, "FACT:...All descriptions of artwork, architecture, documents, and secret rituals in this novel are accurate."[24] Consider, too, the following comment made by Brown during an interview, in which he paints his work as far more factual than fictional:

> One of the many qualities that makes *The Da Vinci Code* unique is the factual nature of the story. All the history, artwork, ancient documents, and secret rituals in the novel are accurate—as are the hidden codes revealed in some of Da Vinci's most famous paintings.[25]

Too many readers of *The Da Vinci Code* have already responded to the novel by trustingly embracing it as historically accurate.

One supporter, for example, posted his views on an Internet fan site, saying, "[T]his book is awesome and confirms many things for me."[26] Another wrote that a "huge amount of information in it is accurate" and that "pretty much all of the historical facts are real."[27]

That Brown's novel would find so many admirers comes as no surprise given the horrific revelations in recent years about priestly misconduct within the Roman Catholic Church, specifically child molestation. University of Southern California historian Richard Fox has explained that Brown "is riding the wave of revulsion against corruption in the Catholic Church." Fox additionally observes, "Really the book is in many ways about how bad the church is."[28]

Right or wrong, *The Da Vinci Code* has clearly struck a spiritual nerve and deserves special attention from those interested in religion. And the primary issue it raises is not even whether or not Christianity is true. Other questions relating to the novel are far more basic:

1. Does it correctly present historical events?
2. Does it properly interpret classic works of art?
3. Does it accurately represent the religious belief systems upon which so much of its plot is based—namely, Christianity and Gnosticism?

Ultimately, the facts should speak for themselves. Therefore, *The Truth Behind The Da Vinci Code* is not a definitive analysis of Brown's novel, but rather a short volume that simply offers verifiable facts in contrast to the bestseller's undocumented assertions. I hope that such an approach will be helpful to those readers who want to reach an informed conclusion about *The Da Vinci Code*.

❖ ❖ ❖

Extrico subjectio quod verum ero evidens.[29]

Chapter 1

Conspiracy Theories, Mass Confusion, and Rewriting History

So error-laden is *The Da Vinci Code* that the educated reader actually applauds those rare occasions where Brown stumbles (despite himself) into the truth.

Sandra Miesel, *Crisis* magazine[1]

It is difficult to know where to begin dissecting *The Da Vinci Code*. Although cleverly written, its overall value is diminished by an unusually high number of factual inaccuracies. For example, Dan Brown asserts that the pyramid outside the Louvre in Paris is "constructed of exactly 666 panes of glass."[2] But according to the official Web site of the Louvre Museum, the pyramid is "covered in 673 diamond-shaped panes of glass."[3] The *Code* also says that the Greeks based their Olympic games on an eight-year cycle as a tribute to the planet Venus, which in those days represented a goddess.[4] In reality, however, the Olympics were held in honor of the Greek god Zeus. And they ran in a four-year, not an eight-year, cycle.

Such mistakes illustrate the book's main weakness—its lack of accuracy, which is especially noticeable in connection to the conspiracy theory it seeks to validate (see introduction). This raises a fascinating point about Brown himself that few people have explored: He seems to be somewhat of a conspiracy buff. All of his previous novels, for instance, have dealt with conspiracies.[5] His next novel, too, will be based on a conspiracy theory—its subject will be Freemasonry, which has long engendered fear and paranoia.

Yet Brown maintains he is not a conspiracy theorist.[6] He claims to be more a "skeptic" than anything else, and he rejects tales of extraterrestrials, crop circles, and "other 'mysteries' that permeate pop culture."[7] Of course, when it comes to conspiracies within Christianity, particularly those related to Roman Catholicism, Brown has been quite willing to accept even the wildest of charges. And he has used his novel to spread them.

Hardly anyone, though, is raising questions about the author's scholarship. Even fewer are verifying his supposed facts. And almost no one has challenged his interpretation of numerous historical events he refers to. A possible explanation for such credulity may lie in the way Brown has presented his story. He relentlessly indicates that authoritative sources support his various claims, naming, for example, "religious historians"; "well-documented history"; "art historians"; "all academics"; "well-documented evidence"; "scores of historians"; and "historical evidence."*

These appeals are suspiciously vague, yet they give the *Code* an air of scholarship and legitimacy. They make it seem as if its assertions are based on exhaustive research that has been corroborated beyond doubt by professionals. Yet this is a false and misleading impression, as the remainder of this chapter will clearly demonstrate.

❖ ❖ ❖

Ancient Symbols

THE DA VINCI CODE:

Pagan symbolism. It is "hidden" in the Chartres Cathedral in Paris (*DVC* page 7).

THE TRUTH BEHIND THE CODE:

There is nothing "hidden" about the pagan symbols at Chartres—which include a labyrinth, a gargoyle, and the great Rose Window. The Church openly used these symbols to attract

---

* Respectively, page 36, pages 88 and 113, page 134, page 158, page 217, page 253, and page 254.

pagans. They were given new Christian meanings so that pagans would, first, feel more at home, and second, better understand what Christianity was trying to say. The labyrinth, for example, was placed *inside* the cathedral because one had existed *outside* the cathedral. Church leaders, after removing the external labyrinth, hoped that pagans might come inside to the new labyrinth, where they could then hear the Christian message.

THE DA VINCI CODE:

The pentacle. This symbol, a five-pointed star within a circle, represents "the female half of all things—a concept religious historians call the 'sacred feminine' or the divine goddess....In its most specific interpretation, the pentacle symbolizes Venus—the goddess of female sexual love and beauty" (*DVC* page 36).

THE TRUTH BEHIND THE CODE:

The pentagram (which is called a pentacle when drawn inside a circle) has no "specific interpretation." Writer and lecturer Kerr Cuhulain, who is a recognized spokesman for Wicca,* explains that "there seems to have been no single tradition concerning their [pentagrams'] meaning and use, and in many contexts they seem simply to have been decorative."[8] Popular Wiccan Doreen Valiente also has noted the pentagram's uses, adding, "The origin of the magical five-pointed star is lost in the mists of time."[9]

The only historical certainty is that in ancient astrology (during the period from about 3000 to 2500 B.C.) the pentagram represented Jupiter, Mercury, Mars, Saturn, and Venus all together—not *just* Venus. The pentagram's relationship to "female sexual love" is tenuous at best. To be sure, Venus was the goddess of sex, fertility, and love—but this has little to do with the pentagram or pentacle *as a whole*.[10]

There is little more information about its other early uses until Pythagoras (about 570 to 495 B.C.), the Greek mathematician. He

---

* According to Webster, Wicca is "a religion influenced by pre-Christian beliefs and practices of western Europe that affirms the existence of supernatural power (as magic) and of both male and female deities who inhere in nature and that emphasizes ritual observance of seasonal and life cycles."

and his followers used the pentagram as their sign, equating it with the Greek word for "health."[11] By 475 B.C., it was being used by the philosopher Empedocles (about 490 to 430 B.C.) for spirit, earth, air, fire, and water: "[T]he star as a whole symbolizes spirit bringing the elements into order and balance."[12]

Today, the pentacle is used mostly by neopagans to indicate the priority of spirituality over materialism. And to them it usually symbolizes *Earth,* not Venus.[13] Satanists also use the symbol, but they draw it upside down to show, among other things, rebellion (see pages 32–33).

THE DA VINCI CODE:

Venus, the Olympics, and the pentagram. The planet Venus traces "a *perfect* pentacle across the ecliptic sky every eight years" (*DVC* page 36). Moreover, "the five-pointed star had almost become the official Olympic seal but was modified at the last moment—its five points exchanged for five intersecting rings" (*DVC* page 37).

THE TRUTH BEHIND THE CODE:

The pentacle did not almost become the "official Olympic seal"—only to lose out to the now-famous rings. The Greeks did not even use the interlocking circles associated with today's games. This design was created in 1913 by the founder of the International Olympic Committee, Baron Pierre de Coubertin.[14] He wanted it to represent the first five Olympic games. The sign's use, however, was delayed until 1920, after which "the ring logo came to symbolize the 'five continents'—a European concept in which North and South America are one."[15]

As for the course of Venus, it does not trace a "perfect" pentacle (or pentagram), but rather an *approximate* pentagram that varies in shape. There is not even "an observation point on Earth that would present a regular pentagram. Moving further north elongates the figure, while on the equator the figure is an irregular pentagon."[16] And this shape is not made by Venus traversing a straight line to each point, as Brown implies.

In order to get a *rough* pentagram out of Venus's course, one must fix the planet's location every 584 days over a period of eight years, then connect the dots. Using these parameters, one would still have to start plotting the positions on very specific days (for example, January 13, 2003). A daily observation—the kind most people would make—would simply show Venus zigzagging back and forth, making a scribble pattern...much like the one that appears on a polygraph test when someone is lying.

THE DA VINCI CODE:

Tarot cards. These occult objects were "devised as a secret means to pass along ideologies banned by the Church" (*DVC* page 92).

THE TRUTH BEHIND THE CODE:

Tarot cards were "originally used for the purpose of divination." It is possible they were invented by Gypsies from the east, who introduced them to Europe in the late 1300s.[17] Another scenario links tarot origins to Muslims, who—unlike Europeans—had playing cards as early as the 1200s. The cards then found their way into Europe, where Gypsies began using and popularizing them.[18] Other scholars trace the tarot to Italy of the early 1400s.[19]

The preceding theories are but a few of the ones that exist about the tarot.[20] Definitive knowledge about how it came about has been lost. All we know is that the card deck appeared in Europe in the late 1300s.[21] As Wiccan Doreen Valiente notes, "No one really knows the origin of the Tarot."[22] Most researchers, however, would probably deny that it was "devised" as a means of spreading "banned" ideologies.

Distortion of the Sacred Past

THE DA VINCI CODE:

Koyaanisqatsi. The Hopi Indians believe that humanity is suffering from *koyaanisqatsi* ("life out of balance"): an instability "marked by testosterone-fueled wars, a plethora of misogynistic societies, and a growing disrespect for Mother Earth" (*DVC* pages 125–126).

THE TRUTH BEHIND THE CODE:

According to the late Thomas Banyacya (died in 1999), who began serving in 1948 as spokesman for Hopi leaders, *koyaanisqatsi* means "life without spirituality, life without sacredness."[23] It has nothing to do with an "obliteration of the sacred feminine" (*DVC* page 125) or male atrocities and misogynistic attitudes.

Koyaanisqatsi relates to a Hopi legend about our loss of spiritual-mindedness. The story is set in the ancient past, at a time when spirituality was replaced by selfishness, materialism, and a lack of appreciation for the sacred and simple. This caused people to grow immoral and destructive. "People had no respect for anything. Life had become *koyaanisqatsi*—a world out of balance."[24] Those affected by *koyaanisqatsi* decided to make a fresh start by leaving their homeland (at that time, the Third World, which was *inside* the earth). So they journeyed through a hole in the sky, which led to where we now live (the Fourth World).[25]

THE DA VINCI CODE:

Suppression of paganism. Christians and pagans were "warring" so fiercely that the conflict "threatened to rend Rome in two. Constantine decided something had to be done. In 325 A.D., he decided to unify Rome under a single religion. Christianity" (*DVC* page 232).

THE TRUTH BEHIND THE CODE:

If the *Code* is implying that Constantine made Christianity the state religion of the Roman Empire in 325, then it is mistaken. Constantine simply granted freedom of worship to Christians (313, the Edict of Milan—see pages 22–25). It was not until 381, during Theodosius' reign (379–395), that Christianity was made the state religion.[26]

As for pagans and Christians "warring" prior to 325, this is partially true. But many pagans and Christians also co-existed quite peacefully.[27] Some pagans—including some Roman officials—actually protected their Christian neighbors from persecutions, especially during the reigns of Decius (249–251), Diocletian (about 284–305), and Galerius (305–311).[28]

And pagan–Christian conflict was hardly the primary threat to the empire. Enemy hordes, for example, were invading the land (the Goths, Vandals, and Huns, among others). Moreover, Roman morality and ethics were eroding. Other factors that led to Rome's downfall included dependence on foreign troops, territorial over-expansion, and political corruption.

THE DA VINCI CODE:

Sunday. "Christianity's weekly holy day was stolen from the pagans. Christianity honored the Jewish Sabbath of Saturday, but Constantine shifted it to coincide with the pagan's veneration day of the sun" (*DVC* pages 232–233).

THE TRUTH BEHIND THE CODE:

Christians *semi*officially adopted Sunday worship during the reign of the Roman emperor Trajan (98–117), who outlawed Saturday—that is, Sabbath—meetings for Christians. However, observance of Sunday as "the Lord's day" is recorded even earlier—in the Bible (Acts 20:7; 1 Corinthians 16:2). Sunday was easily accepted by Christians because it coincided with the Lord's resurrection (Matthew 28:1), his post-resurrection appearances (John 20:26), and the descent of the Holy Spirit (Acts 2:1).

Moreover, references to Sunday as "the Lord's day" appear long before Constantine, in the writings of Justin Martyr (about 100 to 165) and Melito of Sardis (late 100s).[29] The significance of this is underscored by the terminology these writers used: *Sabbath* vs. *Lord's Day*. In other words, although Christians met on "the Lord's day," they still considered Saturday to be the Sabbath. This distinction was noted by the church father Ignatius (died about 110), who explained that the Jewish "Sabbath" was an aspect of the Mosaic Law that had been, for lack of a better term, suspended.[30] No references are made to any hybrid "Christian Sabbath" until the 1100s.[31]

Clearly, if a "Christian Sabbath" did not even exist until the twelfth century, then Constantine could not have "shifted" it to Sunday. He did, however, proclaim in 321 that there should be rest "on the venerable day of the sun." But this merely prohibited "the public disturbance and profanation" of Sunday in order that Christians could worship in peace.[32] In his research, Brown may have misinterpreted this order as a command to shift the Sabbath to Sunday.

Male–Female Deity

THE DA VINCI CODE:

Ritual copulation. "[E]arly Jewish tradition involved ritualistic sex. *In the Temple, no less.* Early Jews believed that the Holy of Holies in Solomon's Temple housed not only God but also His powerful female equal, Shekinah" (*DVC* page 309).

THE TRUTH BEHIND THE CODE:

There are no historical records showing *any* era in Israel when ritualistic sex was sanctioned in the temple. Brown *might* be referring to those sporadic periods in pre-Roman Israel when altars to pagan deities were erected at various locations, contrary to Mosaic Law. But their presence hardly constitutes "Jewish tradition." In facts, these pagan altars were repeatedly torn down by various kings and prophets of Israel (see, for example, Judges 6:25-26,28,30).

Or perhaps the *Code* is referring to those periods in Israel's history (for example, around 900 B.C. and also about the mid-600s B.C.) when the temple was defiled by religious prostitution (see 2 Kings 23:7). However, this abhorrent exploitation of sex was "ritualistic" only within the context of ancient Canaanite fertility religions—not Judaism. In fact, Moses had previously warned Israel to avoid precisely this kind of pagan debauchery (Deuteronomy 23:17-18). True "Jewish tradition," therefore, was actually being followed by the righteous rulers of Israel (for example, Asa, Josiah)—those who sought to *eradicate* ritual sex in the temple, not advocate it (see 1 Kings 15:12; 2 Kings 23:7).

As for *Shekinah,* this is not the name of a goddess, but a combination of Hebrew words that, when linked together, mean "dwelling." The word is not contained in the Bible, although a similar name *(Shecaniah)* is found in 1 Chronicles 3:21. It means "Yahweh dwelling," and it refers to God's presence in the temple. This does not mean that the temple "housed" God. Solomon himself declared that even heaven could not contain God (1 Kings 8:27). Rather, the temple was a place to which people could go to meet God. He had promised to always be there for them.

THE DA VINCI CODE:

God's original name. "The Jewish Tetragrammaton YHWH— the sacred name of God—in fact derived from Jehovah, an androgynous physical union between the masculine *Jah* and the pre-Hebraic name for Eve, *Havah*" (*DVC* page 309).

THE TRUTH BEHIND THE CODE:

Perhaps the only thing truly known about the origin of the tetragrammaton is that the ancient Israelites used it in reference to God. We do not even know its original spelling, nor do we know how it should be pronounced. It *might* have been spelled "Yahweh," but this is uncertain because ancient written Hebrew had no indication of vowels.

The origin of the word *Jehovah* can be traced to the late Middle Ages (around the year 1500), when Jewish scribes began inserting the vowels from the Hebrew word *adonai* ("my Lord") into the name YHWH. The insertion resulted in the hybrid term YaHoWaH. Scribes wanted this new word to remind readers that God's name was too holy to pronounce, so they should substitute *adonah* for it when reading biblical passages aloud. Then, when the term *YaHoWaH* was Latinized, the "Y" and "W" were changed to "J" and "V"—resulting in *Jehovah*.[33]

What about *Havah* (also spelled *Chavvah*)? This is simply the name "Eve" as found in the original Hebrew of the Old Testament. It comes from a root word that means "life." *Havah* has nothing to do with some "androgynous physical union" with "Jah," which is not, as the *Code* says, "masculine." In fact, the term "Jah" is not even a Hebrew word, as noted above. Hebrew, however, does include *Yah,* a contracted form of YHWH. And throughout the Hebrew scriptures, "Yah" is indeed coupled with a masculine verb. In Psalm 106:1, for example, *halal Yah* means "Praise the Lord" or "Praise Yah." Perhaps Brown confused "Yah" with "Jah."

❖ ❖ ❖

The Da Vinci Code clearly contains many historical errors covering a wide variety of issues: church architecture, religious symbolism, the Roman Empire, ancient Israel, and different spiritual belief systems. This is a crucial point because Brown's credibility as a reliable expounder of history is what undergirds many of his assertions about other significant topics, such as the Bible, early church doctrine, and the beliefs embraced by ancient religious groups.

In other words, if Brown cannot be relied upon to accurately recount the most basic of historical facts, then how can he be trusted to correctly explain more complex subjects? Chapter 2 will take a closer look at some of these decidedly intricate topics. At every turn, *The Da Vinci Code*'s "facts" are contradicted by information readily available to any investigator.

Chapter 2

Gnosticism, Ancient Gospels, and the Bible

*The Da Vinci Code [c]ompletely turned my opinion
of the Bible and the Catholic Church upside down.*

A fan of *The Da Vinci Code,* amazon.com,
as quoted in the *Washington Post* [1]

Before looking at the more intricate aspects of *The Da Vinci Code,* we must first know something about the many sources Dan Brown used to build his conspiracy theory. They include numerous works, as widely varied as Leonardo da Vinci's notebooks and twentieth-century bestsellers. Some of his most important texts are the various Gnostic gospels, which he uncritically accepts as accurate accounts of Jesus' life.

As Brown rightly notes, these "gospels" offer an entirely different picture of Christ than the one given in the Bible. This is not surprising, given who their authors are—the *Gnostics.* These early "Christians" not only altered various Christian ideas, but added to them many beliefs associated with other spiritual traditions and religious philosophies.

Gnosticism acquired its name from the Greek term for knowledge (*gnōsis*). Its followers believed that salvation came through "higher knowledge"—that is, divinely revealed truths about the nature of reality. This *gnōsis,* for example, included a revelation that all human souls had originally existed in a spiritual realm of light (*plērōma*) until a tragedy of some kind caused them to start being imprisoned in fleshly bodies on the earth. Flesh, therefore—indeed, all physical matter—was viewed as intrinsically evil.

Gnostic "salvation" equaled liberation of the soul from the body—the freeing of the inner spirit from the confines of matter. Such liberation, however, could only be achieved through *gnōsis*, which brought about detachment from the evil world (similar to Buddhism). To achieve this enlightenment, one needed to *know* the truth about God, himself, and life.[2]

Ancient Gnosticism also preached two gods: a good deity of light and an evil deity of darkness. The good deity (the Principle, or All-Father) was seen as the epitome of love. This God was responsible for having created, not the world we see, but rather, the other god—the one who *did* create the world. This second deity, the evil *demiurge*, seeks only to impede human souls from returning to God and reuniting with the Divine. The good God is utterly removed from the world. He is unknowable.

The All-Father, however, did send a Redeemer—Jesus. But the Gnostic Jesus, unlike the Jesus of Christianity, was not a Savior who died for sins. He was a bringer of *gnōsis*. According to many Gnostics, he also was a completely spiritual being (an *aeon*). These Gnostics believed that he was not truly present in the flesh, because all flesh, all matter, is evil. He may have *appeared* to be physical, but in reality, he was only projecting a phantom body.[3] This Jesus' mission was twofold: 1) to reveal the truth about our "former state—a state that people had forgotten" and point the way back to God; and 2) to "release the divine spark of light imprisoned in matter."[4]

❖ ❖ ❖

The Scriptures and Emperor Constantine

THE DA VINCI CODE:

Constantine's beliefs. "The Bible, as we know it today, was collated by the pagan Roman emperor Constantine....He was a lifelong pagan who was baptized on his deathbed, too weak to protest" (*DVC* pages 231–232). He was the "head priest" of the official Roman religion of sun worship—"the cult of *Sol Invictus*" (*DVC* page 232).

THE TRUTH BEHIND THE CODE:

Constantine (about 274 or 280 to 337) was not a lifelong pagan. According to Kenneth Scott Latourette (1884–1975), Yale professor of Oriental history, Constantine converted to Christianity. This conclusion is accepted by many non-Christian historians and scholars, including those openly critical of Christianity (for example, Elaine Pagels, Princeton University professor of religion, and Keith Hopkins, ancient history professor at King's College).[5]

After his conversion, though, Constantine remained a tolerant emperor, having seen the persecution of Christians. And persecution was something with which he very much disagreed. So rather than use his imperial powers to do the same thing to pagans, he allowed both paganism and Christianity to flourish in freedom under his famous Edict of Milan, or the Edict of Toleration (313). It enabled everyone to "choose whatever religion he preferred."[6]

As for Constantine's position as the "head priest" of the cult of *Sol Invictus,* this is only partially true. His title under that cult—*pontifex maximus*—was more political than anything else. Every emperor was considered by the Roman Senate to be the "head priest" of the state's religion, just as every American president, according to the Constitution, is commander in chief of the armed forces by definition.

Is it not possible that Constantine faked his conversion? It is possible, but not likely. His new faith was evident in his favor toward Christians. He ordered their confiscated property restored, and then called for "financial aid for Catholics, clerical exemption from hereditary offices, civil jurisdiction for bishops."[7] Any ambiguity he may have shown with regard to his new faith must be understood in light of the fact that although he was a Christian, he also was "an absolute monarch ruling an empire still largely pagan."[8] Even today's politicians must be careful about how forcefully they voice their faith.

Moreover, no documentation indicates that Constantine was too weak to protest being baptized on his "deathbed." He was baptized in 337, and until *several days later* wore "the white robes of a neophyte."[9] Why did he wait so long for baptism? It was not from apathy, "but from the conviction, then general, that it [baptism] washed away all previous sins and, being unrepeatable, had best be postponed until as near death as possible."[10]

And Constantine did not collate the Bible. The Old Testament had been compiled even before Jesus' time. As for the New Testament, its formation began by the end of the first century (about 90 or 100)—almost two hundred years before Constantine.[11] During the second century, for example, thousands of quotations from Matthew, Mark, Luke, and John were already being inserted into the writings of church leaders.[12]

By the time of the church father Irenaeus (about 180), "the fourfold character of the Gospel canon had become for orthodox Christians one of the accepted facts of life."[13] By about 230, the well-known Origen (about 185 to 254) had completed a listing of the New Testament books he viewed as authoritative: all four Gospels, Acts, Paul's epistles, 1 Peter, 1 John, and Revelation. He then noted that Hebrews, 2 Peter, 2 and 3 John, James, and Jude were already under consideration for inclusion with the other authoritative books.[14] Other early church writers were also listing, quoting, and discussing the various texts that would eventually become the New Testament.[15] The circulation and discussion of these works continued *throughout* Constantine's rule.

In fact, recognizing which books of the New Testament were authoritative was a centuries-long process within both the Eastern and Western churches.[16] This, too, is a major fact that is missed in *The Da Vinci Code*. There were two major branches of Christianity—one in the east (based at Constantinople) and one in the west (based at Rome). They *independently* agreed on which books should be in the New Testament (both branches had already agreed on the Old Testament).

Documents from this era show a growing consensus about the Bible. Nevertheless, in the Western church an *official* list of the 27 New Testament books was not confirmed until 393 (at the Council of Hippo) and 397 (at the Council of Carthage). In the Eastern church, agreement about the New Testament began solidifying as early as 367. But final confirmation of the books did not occur until later (in the 500s).[17]

Obviously, all these dates are *after* Constantine's death. So what did Constantine have to do with the Bible's collation? Not much—except for a request he made for Eusebius, bishop of Caesarea, to make 50 copies of the Scriptures. Eusebius did so, using *his own list* of widely known texts. He reproduced this list in his work *History of the Church* (about 323 or 325), dividing the texts into three groups: accepted, disputed, and rejected.[18] These groups included all of the works in today's New Testament and the Greek version of the Old Testament.

THE DA VINCI CODE:

No definitive Bible. The Christian Scriptures "evolved through countless translations, additions, and revisions. History has never had a definitive version of the book" (*DVC* page 231).

THE TRUTH BEHIND THE CODE:

We have just had a brief overview of how we arrived at today's "definitive version" of the Bible (see pages 24–25).[19] As for the Bible's reliability, both the Old and New Testaments are well supported by copies that have been extensively compared and contrasted. The New Testament is especially well-established by existing manuscripts. Moreover, many copies of these copies are dated very close to the composition of the originals (for example, one fragment of John's Gospel dates back to the emperor Hadrian's reign, 117–138).

It is widely recognized by scholars that the closer an original document or a manuscript copy can be dated to the event it describes, the more likely it is to be reliable. Biblical studies professor F.F. Bruce noted, "If the New Testament were a collection of secular writings, their authenticity would generally be regarded as beyond all doubt."[20] Support for this statement is easily obtained by making a simple comparison of the manuscripts and manuscript fragments of the New Testament (there exist nearly 5600 Greek copies alone). Although they contain many *minor* variants, these copies have helped narrow the text down to a version that is undoubtedly very close to the originals.[21]

THE DA VINCI CODE:

Rewriting the Scriptures. Constantine "commissioned and financed a new Bible, which omitted those gospels that spoke of Christ's *human* traits and embellished those gospels that made Him godlike. The earlier gospels were outlawed, gathered up and burned" (*DVC* page 234).

THE TRUTH BEHIND THE CODE:

There is no historical evidence showing that Matthew, Mark, Luke, and John were "embellished" by Constantine, Eusebius (see pages 24–25), or any of Eusebius's scribes. Moreover, the Gospels hardly ignore Christ's "*human* traits." Christians believe that Jesus was 100-percent divine *and* 100-percent human. Therefore, erasing the elements of his humanity would have been contrary to what the church was teaching in Constantine's day. Aspects of Jesus' humanity recorded in the Gospels include his amazement (Matthew 8:10), his anger (Mark 11:15-16), his hunger and fatigue (Luke 4:2; 8:23), and his sorrow (John 11:33-36).

Although the additional indictment against Constantine for destroying *earlier* gospels is a bit unclear, the use of the word "burned" is a clue to what Dan Brown may have had in mind. He might be referring to Constantine's edict of the year 325, calling for the writings of Arius to be burned. Arius's teachings, which conflicted with the conclusions of many church leaders about what the New Testament was saying, caused a great debate at the Council of Nicaea (325)—a debate that ended with his views being rejected.

But contrary to what the *Code* may be indicating, none of Arius's writings were *gospels*—least of all, Gnostic ones. His books and letters consisted primarily of detailed doctrinal arguments relating to the nature of Jesus Christ: whether or not he was a created being. Though Constantine wanted Arius's writings destroyed, he gave no orders against either pagan works or Gnostic gospels.

But were the Gnostic gospels written *prior to* the books of Matthew, Mark, Luke, and John? Most scholars, Christian and non-Christian, would answer no. They date the Gnostic gospels (for example, those in the Nag Hammadi collection—see page 28) to about A.D. 250 to 350. Although many of these texts are Coptic translations of *earlier* Greek texts (that are no longer extant), most scholars agree that the material itself still does not date previous to the mid 100s to early 200s.[22]

In other words, the Gnostic texts were written after the books of Matthew (about 65 to 100), Mark (about 40 to 75), Luke (about 60 to 80), and John (about 90). They were late arrivals, which is one reason why church leaders rejected them.[23] Criticism of these works appears as early as the second century (for instance, Irenaeus, about 180).[24] These Gnostic gospels not only disagreed with the older Gospels, which were already accepted by Christians, but they lacked authority since their authors were neither a) apostles of Jesus nor b) persons associated with apostles of Jesus.

This sheds light on another flaw in Brown's exaltation of the Gnostic gospels—they were not written by those persons whose names are attached to them. These names—Mary, Philip, Thomas, and others—are pseudonyms. No one really knows who wrote the texts.

THE DA VINCI CODE:

Defining "heretic." "Anyone who chose the forbidden gospels over Constantine's version was deemed a heretic. The word *heretic* derives from that moment in history. The Latin word *haereticus* means 'choice.' Those who 'chose' the original history of Christ [those gospels rejected by Constantine] were the world's first *heretics*" (*DVC* page 234).

THE TRUTH BEHIND THE CODE:

Once again the *Code* falsely attributes Eusebius's work—his list of accepted gospels—to Constantine. Moreover, it erroneously claims that the word *heretic* derived "from that moment in history" (about 313 to 325). In reality, the word appears much earlier—in the New Testament book of Titus, which was written by the apostle Paul about A.D. 63 to 64. Paul's admonition was to reject anyone who was heretical (*hairetikos,* Titus 3:10). The Greek word for heresy *(hairesis)* shows up even earlier, in 1 Corinthians 11:19 (about 54). Further, both terms can be found well before the time of Constantine in the writings of Irenaeus (his "Irenaeus Against Heresies," about 182 to 188) and Tertullian (his "Prescription Against Heretics," around the late 100s).

The Destruction of the "Older" Gospels

THE DA VINCI CODE:

Finding the scrolls. Some of the gospels Constantine tried to destroy "managed to survive. The Dead Sea Scrolls were found in the 1950s....And, of course, the Coptic Scrolls in 1945 at Nag Hammadi." Further, "the Vatican, in keeping with their tradition of misinformation, tried very hard to suppress the release of these scrolls....These are...[t]he earliest Christian records" (*DVC* pages 234, 245).

THE TRUTH BEHIND THE CODE:

Why the Dead Sea Scrolls are mentioned here is a mystery since they contain no "gospels" of any kind.[25] The manuscripts, which are *pre-Christian Jewish,* include portions of every Old Testament book (except Esther), commentaries on the Old Testament, extrabiblical works, secular documents, and business records. The Qumran community, which wrote or preserved these scrolls, had nothing to do with Jesus or Christianity. It was an isolationist sect that apparently split from the Jewish Essenes (a Jewish monastic order that existed from about 200 B.C. to A.D. 200).[26] Not one of the Qumran manuscripts can be dated to later than A.D. 68. Most of them, in fact, were written centuries before Christ.

As for the Nag Hammadi collection, it does indeed contain several gospels that are Gnostic in origin. But the assertion that "the Vatican" tried to suppress their publication is unfounded. According to James M. Robinson, director of the Institute for Antiquity and Christianity and Claremont Graduate School, it took until 1977 to publish the manuscripts in English because "[s]cholarly rivalries and the situation in Egypt in the years following the library's discovery in 1945 hindered the work on the manuscripts."[27]

Finally, it should be noted that the gospels found at Nag Hammadi, contrary to the *Code,* are *not* the "earliest Christian records." As previously noted (see page 26), the physical copies that were found date to about 250 to 350, while the Greek originals on which the copies were based were composed no earlier than the mid 100s to the early 200s.

THE DA VINCI CODE:

The revision of Jesus' life. "[A]ny gospels that described *earthly* aspects of Jesus' life had to be omitted from the Bible" (*DVC* page 244).

THE TRUTH BEHIND THE CODE:

The Gospels in today's Bible, as we saw earlier, include many *"earthly* aspects" of Jesus' life. They show his physical limitations (hunger, fatigue, death), his human emotions (anguish, sadness, outrage), and his relational interactions (with his mother, friends, followers). So what is being referred to? Nothing more than an absence in the Gospels of Jesus' sexuality. This is a major premise of *The Da Vinci Code:* namely, since the Gospels do not show Jesus in a sexual relationship of some kind (for example, a marriage), then they are not representing him as truly human and earthly. They are giving a false picture of who he was.

There is an enormous problem with this kind of thinking. Must someone be married or sexually active to be "earthly"? Hardly. Neither celibacy nor having no spouse makes anyone less human or earthly. But for some reason, when it comes to Jesus, the *Code* portrays singleness as being incompatible with what it means to be human and earthly.

❖ ❖ ❖

The interaction between Gnosticism and Christianity has always been a fascinating subject and is worthy of careful study. Dan Brown's version of this interaction, however, not only contradicts the historical record, but it also disagrees with modern assessments of that period in history. And as we have seen, associated with this problem is a complete misrepresentation of one of the most basic aspects of Christianity—the formation of the Bible, including the collation of both the New and Old Testaments.

Contrary to *The Da Vinci Code,* the Bible has a very clear and well-defined history. And many honorable and respected scholars have embraced the traditional Christian belief that the Old and New Testaments together create a remarkable record of God's dealings with humanity.[28] Like these respected academics, traditional

Christians have found sufficient evidence to historically support what the Bible itself claims to be: the very Word of God.[29]

The Da Vinci Code, on the other hand, paints the Bible as little more than a fraudulent compilation of texts initially used by scurrilous deceivers bent on controlling the masses. As much of a distortion as this may be, even more troubling is Brown's misappropriation of some key figures of the Christian church in the attempt to validate his conspiracy theory: namely, Mary Magdalene and Jesus Christ. They will be the subject of chapter 3.

Chapter 3

Mary Magdalene, the Church, and Goddess Worship

If you know someone who was upset by Martin Scorsese's film The Last Temptation of Christ, The Da Vinci Code *should make them fall down frothing at the mouth.*

Charles Taylor, book review, salon.com[1]

Central to the *The Da Vinci Code* is the figure of Mary Magdalene. Equally pivotal are first-century pagan beliefs, Jewish traditions, and early church doctrines. Particularly crucial is the alleged marriage of Jesus to Magdalene, and their alleged devotion to the sacred feminine (or the goddess). Did the early church distort Christ's message? Who was Mary Magdalene? How did the church view her? Was there a conspiracy to cover up her identity?

Although it has been shown that Dan Brown's overall scholarship is questionable, this still does not necessarily disprove his assertions about 1) Magdalene's relationship to Jesus, 2) actions taken by the early and modern church regarding goddess worship, 3) Mary's possible role as Christ's successor, or 4) the development of various Christian doctrines.

❖ ❖ ❖

Eliminating
the "Sacred Feminine"

THE DA VINCI CODE:

Misrepresentation of divine symbols. "As part of the Vatican's campaign to eradicate pagan religions and convert the masses to Christianity, the Church launched a smear campaign against the pagan gods and goddesses, recasting their divine symbols as evil....Venus's pentacle became the sign of the devil" (*DVC* page 37).

THE TRUTH BEHIND THE CODE:

The most striking aspect of this statement is its inconsistency with a later remark in the *Code*. To see the inconsistency, we need only compare the above quote from page 37 to page 232. On the former page, the Church is excoriated for recasting paganism's "divine symbols" as evil. But then on page 232 the complaint suddenly changes. Here the Church is condemned for accepting pagan symbols and reassigning Christian beliefs to them. According to Brown, this proves that Christianity is but a poor copy of older and far richer systems of spirituality.[2]

The *Code* has thus put the Church in a no-win situation. In other words, if the Church represents pagan symbols as evil, that is bad. If the Church accepts pagan symbols as harmless and tries to use or transform them, that also is bad. Brown gives the Church no opportunity to avoid a negative evaluation. And this artificial dilemma is constructed at the expense of historical accuracy.

Consider, for example, the denunciation of the Church for transforming the pentacle or pentagram into "a sign of the devil" (*DVC* page 37). The truth is, during the later medieval era (the 1100s to the 1500s), Christians used the pentagram and pentacle as a reminder of Christ's five wounds (hands, feet, side, back, head). They also used it as a symbol for "the five books of Moses" and "the five stones used by David against Goliath."[3]

No one seems to know for sure when the pentagram and pentacle began to be linked with the devil. For centuries it was used by both pagans and Christians in the belief that it could ward off evil spirits. Ironically, the one person responsible for poisoning public perceptions of the pentagram and pentacle was probably Eliphas Levi (1810–1875), a French occultist.

Many neopagans and witches trace the anti-pentacle view to Levi, saying, for instance, "It was Eliphas Levi in the nineteenth century who started the idea that the inverted pentagram was a symbol for Satan."[4] The notion was then cemented in the public's mind when Anton LaVey (1930–1997), who founded the Church of Satan in 1966, chose the pentacle to symbolize his religion. (Among Satanists, the pentagram or pentacle is usually depicted upside down with a goat's head in the center. This symbol is called the Baphomet.)

THE DA VINCI CODE:

The campaign against the goddess. Constantine and his successors "converted the world from matriarchal paganism to patriarchal Christianity by waging a campaign of propaganda that demonized the sacred feminine, obliterating the modern goddess from religion" (*DVC* page 124).

THE TRUTH BEHIND THE CODE:

Ancient paganism was neither matriarchal nor patriarchal. It was not even close to a unified belief system. Those adhering to various *forms* of paganism often revered "dozens or hundreds of gods, goddesses, spirits, and less easily defined supernatural entities."[5] Instead of there being any single "matriarchal paganism," there actually existed *many different paganisms.* Some did not even involve a goddess.[6]

The kind of all-pervading goddess that *The Da Vinci Code* exalts is a relatively recent concept. It began to evolve thanks to the Greek Platonists (from about 300 B.C. to A.D. 200), whose philosophical musings developed the theory that nature was "a living, quasi-divine being, mediating between the transcendent world of Ideas and the realm of matter."[7]

This speculation continued to morph until the early 1800s, when the modern neopagan depiction of the mother-goddess (or sacred feminine) entered the poetry of the romantic era. Then, in the early 1900s, the English classicist Jane Harrison voiced the notions now parroted in the *Code* (see endnote for more explanation).[8] Her views were dispersed by the English poet Robert Graves

(1895–1985), whose book *The White Goddess* (1948) became "the most influential source of Goddess imagery and ideology for the modern pagan revival."[9]

In what was almost a foreshadowing of *The Da Vinci Code,* many readers of *The White Goddess* thought Graves was relating historical fact in his work. In reality, he was using the "matriarchies of old Europe and their suppression by patriarchal invaders" to depict his own life, his personal take on reality, and the nature of poetic mythmaking.[10] In the *Code,* noteworthy is not only the repetition of Harrison and Graves's basic idea, but the departure from it. Instead of blaming prehistoric "patriarchal invaders,"[11] Brown blames the Church—a more modern spin on the original Harrison and Graves story.

As for the oldest civilizations (for example, Sumerians, Canaanites, Assyrians, and Egyptians), they never relied exclusively on goddess worship. Their goddesses (Anat, Asherah, Astarte, and so on) were always mated to male deities. Abundant evidence supports this fact. For instance, an Egyptian *stele* (commemorative carved stone) from a temple built by Ramses III[12] depicts the goddess Anat as "the queen of heaven, the mistress of all the gods."[13]

Another thing Brown fails to mention is that many of the earliest fertility goddesses were goddesses of war, death, or both. Anat, for instance, was a Canaanite goddess "of violence and sexuality,"[14] whose "bloodthirsty nature is shockingly explicit in one well-known text...in which she is described as joyously wading thigh-deep in the blood of slain warriors."[15] In this scene "Anat fastens severed heads and hands to her waist."[16]

The Witch Hunts

THE DA VINCI CODE:

The Inquisition and women. The *Malleus Maleficarum* ("hammer of witches"), published by the Inquisition (an arm of the Roman Catholic Church), "indoctrinated the world to 'the dangers of freethinking women' and instructed the clergy how to locate, torture, and destroy them" (*DVC* page 125).

THE TRUTH BEHIND THE CODE:

The *Code*'s references to the *Malleus Maleficarum* (1486) and the "witch hunts" it spawned are filled with error. This medieval book, for example, was used to persecute both women *and men*.[17] Moreover, the use of quotation marks to imply that the words "the dangers of freethinking women" can be found in the *Malleus Maleficarum* is misleading. The phrase actually appears nowhere in its text.

THE DA VINCI CODE:

Persecution of so-called witches. Those hunted down by the Church "included all female scholars, priestesses, gypsies, mystics, nature lovers, herb gatherers, and any women 'suspiciously attuned to the natural world.' Midwives also were killed for their heretical practice of using medical knowledge to ease the pain of childbirth" (*DVC* page 125).

THE TRUTH BEHIND THE CODE:

Countless women in the groupings listed in the *Code* were never targets of persecution by the Church. The comment about midwives also is untrue. Women practiced midwifery and herbal medicine all over medieval Europe without fear. In fact, many midwives and healers (for example, the well-known Hildegard von Bingen, born 1098) were Roman Catholic.[18]

The truth is, women *and men* from all walks of life were subject to persecution under the *Malleus Maleficarum:* priests, nuns, artists, transients, political enemies, social outcasts, rival neighbors, and others.[19] It is simplistic and highly inaccurate to say that the witch hunts were merely an attempt by Church leaders to eradicate paganism and suppress women. As one scholar has noted, "No one explanation or theory will suffice to explain all Witch Hunts in Europe from 1400 to 1800."[20]

In fact, historical documents show that most of the victims "were not killed by Catholics or officials of the Church," but were executed by the state.[21] "'The vast majority of witches were condemned by secular courts, with local courts especially noted for their persecutory zeal.'"[22]

THE DA VINCI CODE:

The number of victims. "During three hundred years of witch hunts, the Church burned at the stake an astounding five *million* women" (*DVC* page 125).

THE TRUTH BEHIND THE CODE:

Scholarly estimates put the number of "witch hunt" victims in Europe from 1400 to 1800 (a period 100 years longer than the 300 years the *Code* mentions) at 30,000 to 80,000.[23] At most, there were probably no more than 100,000 victims.[24] Even some neopagans and witches cite figures as low as 50,000.[25] Moreover, "20 to 25 percent of Europeans executed for witchcraft between the 14th and 17th centuries were male."[26]

It also should be noted that these persecutions were actually "a collaborative enterprise between men and women at the local level."[27] Adam Jones, professor of international studies at the Center for Research and Teaching in Economics (Mexico City), has cited many sources showing that most of the accusations of witchcraft "originated in 'conflicts [that] normally opposed one woman to another.'"[28]

For instance, Jones quotes Robin Briggs (author of *Witches & Neighbours: The Social and Cultural Context of European Witchcraft*) as saying that "most informal accusations were made by women against other women."[29] In *Malevolent Nurture,* Deborah Willis of the University of California, Riverside, confirms that "women were actively involved in making witchcraft accusations against their female neighbors."[30] She adds, "To a considerable extent, then, village-level witch-hunting was women's work."[31]

Dan Brown presents none of these facts in *The Da Vinci Code.* Instead, he unleashes a radical feminist version of the tragedy upon his readers. As Deborah Willis notes, such polemical accounts "are likely to portray the witch as a heroic proto-feminist resisting patriarchal oppression and a wholly innocent victim of a male-authored reign of terror designed to keep women in their place."[32]

Jesus and Women

THE DA VINCI CODE:

A vote on Jesus' divinity. It was at the Council of Nicaea in 325 that Church leaders decided by vote to make Jesus divine. "[U]ntil that moment in history, Jesus was viewed by His followers as a mortal prophet" (*DVC* page 233).

THE TRUTH BEHIND THE CODE:

The Council of Nicaea had nothing to do with *deciding* Jesus' divinity. The most pressing issue before it involved a man named Arius (see pages 26–27), who was teaching that Jesus was a created being.

It is critical to note that, by the end of his earthly ministry, Christ's divinity was already being acknowledged, as evidenced by the words of Thomas to Jesus: "My Lord and my God" (John 20:28). Other passages in the Bible that ascribe divinity to Jesus include John 1:1, Titus 2:13, Hebrews 1:8-10, and 2 Peter 1:1.

By the end of the second century, this belief was firmly held by Christians. Consider the following descriptions of Jesus:

- *Justin Martyr* (about 150): "being the first-begotten Word of God, is even God"; "both God and Lord of hosts" [33]

- *Irenaeus* (about 185): "our Lord, and God, and Saviour, and King"[34]

- *Clement of Alexandria* (about 200): "truly most manifest Deity, He that is made equal to the Lord of the universe; because he was His Son"[35]

THE DA VINCI CODE:

Eve's role in the "Fall." The Church "demonized" the sacred feminine and the goddess by teaching the concept of original sin, "whereby Eve tasted the apple and caused the downfall of the human race" (*DVC* page 238).

THE TRUTH BEHIND THE CODE:

Christianity does not declare that Eve caused humanity's downfall. The church teaches that the Fall came through Eve *and Adam*—particularly Adam because he deliberately chose to disobey God. Hence, the Bible teaches that "since by *a man* came death, by a man also came the resurrection....For as *in Adam* all die, so also in Christ all will be made alive" (1 Corinthians 15:21-22, emphasis added). It is true that some early church leaders did speak of human bondage coming through Eve's actions. But this was not to degrade women. Rather, such remarks were usually made in conjunction with praises for the Virgin Mary's obedience to God. Her actions were contrasted with Eve's—and this comparison reflected the Bible's contrast of Jesus with Adam.[36]

THE DA VINCI CODE:

The threat of the feminine. Leaders of the "predominantly male" Church were so threatened by the power of women's reproductive capabilities that they labeled the sacred feminine and the goddess as unclean. "Woman, once the sacred giver of life, was now the enemy" (*DVC* page 238).

THE TRUTH BEHIND THE CODE:

Woman, according to Christianity, is not man's "enemy." Genesis 2:18-25 tells us that woman is actually the indispensable helper of man and worthy of honor. Jesus and his early followers consistently sought to demonstrate this truth and elevate women to a place of equality with men. For example, women were given direct access to Christ while he gave his sermons (Luke 10:38-39). This broke with Hebrew tradition, which called for a rigid separation of men and women in religious contexts—usually to the exclusion of women from various freedoms and blessings enjoyed by men, such as personal access to a rabbi like Jesus.

THE DA VINCI CODE:

Jesus' marriage. "One particularly troubling theme kept recurring in the [Gnostic] gospels. Mary Magdalene....More specifically, her marriage to Jesus Christ" (*DVC* page 244).

THE TRUTH BEHIND THE CODE:

None of the Gnostic gospels within the Nag Hammadi library— the *Gospel of Truth,* the *Gospel of Thomas,* the *Gospel of Philip*—contain any references to a marriage between Mary Magdalene and Jesus. The *Gospel of Mary* also is silent on the issue.

THE DA VINCI CODE:

Jesus' companion. The Gospel of Philip says that "'the companion of the Savior is Mary Magdalene. Christ loved her more than all the disciples and used to kiss her often on her mouth. The rest of the disciples were offended by it and expressed disapproval. They said to him, "Why do you love her more than all of us?"'...As any Aramaic scholar will tell you, the word *companion,* in those days, literally meant *spouse"* (*DVC* page 246).

THE TRUTH BEHIND THE CODE:

The *Gospel of Philip* is not written in Aramaic. It is written in Coptic—a late form of Egyptian. And even this is a translation of an earlier text in Greek, not Aramaic. Moreover, according to professor Craig Blomberg of Denver Seminary, "no Aramaic or Hebrew words for 'companion' normally mean spouse!"[37] Margaret Mitchell, professor of early church history at the University of Chicago Divinity School, essentially agrees. According to Mitchell, the *Code* is using "a shaky translation" of a word that "is usually translated as friend or companion."[38]

THE DA VINCI CODE:

The Jewish view of marriage. Jesus being a married man makes "infinitely more sense than our standard biblical view of Jesus" because "the social decorum during that time virtually forbid a Jewish man to be unmarried" (*DVC* page 245).

THE TRUTH BEHIND THE CODE:

It is true that during Old Testament times men were expected to marry. By Jesus' era, however, the Jews had become more flexible about marriage. John the Baptist, for example, remained single. And in 1 Corinthians 7:8, the apostle Paul encourages single believers to remain in that condition, "even as I." In this chapter, Paul deals specifically with celibacy, actually endorsing it as a "gift" that is given to some people.

THE DA VINCI CODE:

Mary Magdalene and church leadership. The *Gospel of Mary* (Magdalene) reveals that Mary was given instructions by Jesus "on how to carry on His Church....As a result, Peter expresses his discontent over playing second fiddle to a woman." According to the "unaltered" *Gospel of Mary* and *Gospel of Philip,* "it was not Peter to whom Christ gave directions with which to establish the Christian Church. It was *Mary Magdalene*" (*DVC* pages 247–248).

THE TRUTH BEHIND THE CODE:

Regarding the second-century *Gospel of Mary,* we must note that it is not part of the Nag Hammadi manuscripts (as the *Code* implies elsewhere). Only three small fragments of it exist: two very short fragments copied in about the third century (in Greek), and a slightly longer fragment copied in the fifth century (in Coptic).

The portion cited in the *Code* is partially from the Greek fragments and partially from the Coptic fragment.[39] But they actually say nothing about Mary being chosen to take over the Church. Nor do they reveal that Mary was Jesus' spouse. The fragments simply say that 1) Jesus loved Mary "more than the rest of women" and "more than" the other apostles, and that 2) Jesus shared with Mary certain truths he did not share with his other disciples.

And the actual *Gospel of Mary* message that Jesus allegedly imparted—which Brown omits from the *Code*—has nothing to do with church leadership. It is about metaphysical "powers" and the forms they take to conquer the soul—such as ignorance and wrath. Moreover, Peter does not express irritation over his leadership role, or lack thereof. In the Gnostic text, he challenges

Magdalene's claims because, as another apostle says, "these teachings are strange ideas."[40]

As for the *Gospel of Philip*, it also says nothing about Jesus ordaining Mary Magdalene to take over for him. The text is primarily about "the meaning and value of sacraments" within the Gnostic paradigm.[41] Ironically, if this text does anything, it cuts out the very heart of any assertion about Mary and Jesus being wed. It does so by adhering to one of the basic tenets of ancient Gnosticism, which declares that all physical matter was inherently evil. Consequently, sexual relations were intrinsically debasing!

The *Gospel of Philip* goes so far as to say that marital relations *defile* a woman. As Wesley Isenberg, translator of the *Gospel of Philip,* explains, "'Defiled women' are all women who participate in sexual intercourse, i.e., in 'marriage of defilement,' which is fleshly and lustful (81,34-29; 85,24)."[42]

Christ's Descendants

THE DA VINCI CODE:

The documentation of Jesus' lineage. "The royal bloodline of Jesus Christ has been chronicled in exhaustive detail by scores of historians" (*DVC* page 253).

THE TRUTH BEHIND THE CODE:

Dan Brown clearly hopes to add scholarly weight and an air of credibility to his assertion about Jesus' bloodline by using the word "historians." Following this, four books are listed: *Holy Blood, Holy Grail* (Michael Baigent, Richard Leigh, Henry Lincoln), *The Woman with the Alabaster Jar* (Margaret Starbird), *The Goddess in the Gospels* (Margaret Starbird), and *The Templar Revelation* (Lynn Picknett and Clive Prince).

But none of these authors are, in fact, historians. Starbird holds an M.A. in comparative literature and German. Baigent has an undergraduate degree in psychology and has recently been pursuing an M.A. in Mysticism and Religious Experience. And Leigh "is primarily a novelist and writer of short stories."[43] What about Lincoln? He is a BBC television personality and scriptwriter.[44] And

Picknett and Prince are actually conspiracy theorists with a penchant for occultism, the paranormal, and UFOs.[45]

THE DA VINCI CODE:

The Merovingians. "Christ's line grew quietly under cover in France until making a bold move in the fifth century, when it intermarried with French royal blood and created a lineage known as the Merovingian bloodline....The Merovingians founded Paris" (*DVC* page 257).

THE TRUTH BEHIND THE CODE:

Paris was founded by a Celtic people, the Gauls, and specifically the tribe of the Parisii, who "settled there between 250 and 200 B.C."[46] The city became part of the Roman Empire after being conquered in 52 B.C. by Julius Caesar. The Merovingians did not even exist at this time. They showed up hundreds of years later, when the area was taken over by the Franks, a union of western *Germanic* tribes.[47] These tribes migrated to Belgic Gaul about A.D. 200 to 250, and under King Clovis I (481–511), they seized control of the area now called France in about 486.

The beginnings of the Merovingian lineage can be traced to King Merovech, who ruled from about 447 to 457—long before the Franks entered the Paris region. It was his grandson, Clovis I, who chose the *already existing* city of Paris for his capital.

THE DA VINCI CODE:

Mary Magdalene's reputation. In order to eradicate the truth about Jesus' marriage, the Church "outlawed speaking of the shunned Mary Magdalene," which forced her followers to pass on the truth through "more discreet channels" (*DVC* page 261).

THE TRUTH BEHIND THE CODE:

Magdalene was never "shunned." The Bible explains that it was she who came to tell the disciples about Christ's resurrection

(John 20:17-18). She also is pictured meeting the risen Lord (John 20:11-17).

Unfortunately, Pope Gregory I (540–604) confused Magdalene with "the woman who was a sinner" in Luke 7:37. This led to a false impression of her in the Western church. But Eastern church leaders and theologians never accepted Gregory's view. Even in the Western church in the late 1200s, Dominican priests devoted themselves to Magdalene and initiated the Feast of St. Mary Magdalene in 1297.[48] Though Western church leaders may have been confused about Magdalene's identity, speaking about her (either in the West or in the East) certainly was never "outlawed."

❖ ❖ ❖

It is true that some aspects of early Christianity are still a mystery. For example, we do not know precisely what happened to some New Testament persons, such as Mary Magdalene and many of the apostles. But there are certain things we do know, especially about how early Christians viewed Jesus. Not only is there an absence of material to support *The Da Vinci Code*'s claims, but there actually exists a wealth of information contradicting Dan Brown's conspiracy notions.

Contrary to Brown's ideas, there was no conspiracy to make Jesus "divine." Indeed, there was no need for such a conspiracy. From the earliest years of Christianity, Jesus' followers saw him as the promised Messiah. The Jews who chose to reject Jesus understood very well his claims, which they described as making himself out to be God (John 10:33). He not only claimed to be divine by virtue of his self-professed power and authority (Matthew 13:41; 25:31-34; Mark 2:5; Luke 5:20), but also demonstrated his divinity by raising himself from the dead (John 2:19-22). And as mentioned, Scripture presents none other than Mary Magdalene as the first eyewitness to this miraculous event (John 20:17-18).

Chapter 4

The Grail,
the Priory of Sion, and
the Knights Templar

[A] great deal of information has been published in books like *Holy Blood,
Holy Grail* alleging that the Holy Grail actually refers to a bloodline descended
from Jesus. Well-intentioned readers and even authors have been deceived
by this story and have mistaken it for the revelation of a suppressed history.
Unfortunately, the only thing that has been suppressed is the truth.

Robert Richardson (1999), in *Gnosis: A Journal of the Western Inner Traditions*[1]

Rumor, gossip, and propaganda. They are powerful tools in the
hands of those who know how to wield them. As Mark Pesce, co-
inventor of virtual reality for the Internet, has stated, "In the
wrong mouths, words can lead to disaster. Consider Jim Jones or
Adolph Hitler, who, by force of their oratory, led hundreds and
millions to their deaths."[2]

Yet words can often be rendered powerless—especially false
words. All it takes is just a little truth to dissolve them into a mist
that simply drifts away. This is apparent when it comes to so
many of the claims made in *The Da Vinci Code* concerning the
Holy Grail, the Priory of Sion, and the Knights Templar. This
chapter will reveal that there does exist a conspiracy of sorts
involving these issues...but it is not the one presented in Dan
Brown's novel.

❖ ❖ ❖

The Holy Grail

THE DA VINCI CODE:

The Grail's most ancient meaning. Although the term for Holy Grail has usually been written *San Greal* (from Old French), "[i]n its most ancient form" it was divided as *"Sang Real...Royal Blood"* (*DVC* page 250).

THE TRUTH BEHIND THE CODE:

The earliest reference to the Holy Grail is simply *Graal* ("Grail"),* not *Sang Real* ("royal blood"). The latter form originated in the late Middle Ages (1400s to 1500s), when Christians believed that the Grail (the cup used by Christ at the Last Supper) had been used by Joseph of Arimathea at the crucifixion to catch the "holy blood" of Jesus.

The first allusion to this object appears in *Perceval* (about 1170), an unfinished work by Chrétien de Troyes, a medieval writer of Arthurian romance poems and stories. He seems to have based his tale primarily on Celtic myths. The *Perceval* story revolves around a young man who must prove himself worthy of being a knight.

His adventures lead him to a castle where he sees a procession in which a damsel enters "holding between her two hands a grail...of refined gold...set with precious stones of many kinds."[3] The Grail is only part of a larger procession that also includes a blood-tipped spear and a carving platter of silver.[4] It is not the focus of the story.

The next forty years of the medieval era (about 1180 to 1220) inspired "nearly the entire body of grail stories that still survive."[5] These tales include an anonymous continuation of *Perceval* titled *The High History of the Holy Grail* (early 1200s) and German poet Wolfram von Eschenbach's *Parsifal* (1207).[6] Eventually, all of the Arthurian stories relating to the Holy Grail became more Christianized, until the Grail was linked to Christ.

Nowhere in this literature is there any hint of the Holy Grail being a person. And it must not be forgotten that the initial tales

---

* *Graal* is probably derived from the Latin *gradale,* a type of serving dish.

were drawn from pagan myths, such as *Peredur,* which was part of a collection of Welsh legends known as the Mabinogion. *Perceval,* in fact, is almost a plagiarized *Peredur*—except in the pagan Welsh myth the Grail is a deep platter holding the head of a slain kinsman.

THE DA VINCI CODE:

The symbols for female and "chalice." The icons for male ♂ (and the planet Mars) and female ♀ (and the planet Venus) "are not the original symbols for male and female" (*DVC* page 237). The *original* symbols were ⋀ and ⋁. The latter sign is a chalice (or cup), and as such, refers to the Grail—that is, Mary Magdalene.

THE TRUTH BEHIND THE CODE:

There was no "original" female sign. And the signs that *were* used do not match *The Da Vinci Code*'s: for example, ♀ and ⊕ (ancient Greece).[7] The three oldest and most popular goddess figures (Venus, Ishtar, Astarte) were pictured with a ✳.[8] We also have ▽, which denoted a woman "in prehistoric times and was used by the Sumerians (c. 3000 B.C.)."[9] Another sign used during this era was ⋁.[10] It probably evolved into Υ , which, when inverted, symbolized a male.[11] Finally, there is ℩, which was used by the Egyptians for the "uterus of a heifer, and was first used to signify cow and vulva."[12] This sign most closely resembles the one used in the *Code.* But why would Magdalene be associated with an Egyptian cow?

As for the symbol for a man, it is indeed ♂. However, throughout history it has been drawn as ⟍,[13] as well as ⌀ (a Greek symbol for the god Ares)[14] and ᛘ (a Nordic rune)[15]—not ⋀. Brown's "original" male sign is actually a *chevron,* which has always been used "in military and heraldic contexts."[16] As far back as 3000 B.C., ⫸ can be found "on the clothes of high-ranking chiefs."[17] It meant military rank, not maleness.

Bluntly put, the *Code* fails to accurately depict two of the most common of all symbols. Moreover, such symbols were often merged. For example, Υ was used in centuries past as a sign for the Virgin Mary *as well as* for a man![18]

THE DA VINCI CODE:

What the Grail represents. The Holy Grail, or chalice, is a metaphor for Magdalene (*DVC* pages 162, 244). In fact, the ancient female symbol ∨ is called a *chalice*—and this "chalice" symbol, because it resembles the shape of a woman's womb, conveys "femininity, womanhood, and fertility" (*DVC* page 238). The description of the Holy Grail as a chalice was "actually an allegory" used to protect the identity of Mary Magdalene—who was the true Holy Grail (*DVC* page 238). She was the "Holy Vessel" trusted to bear the royal bloodline of Christ (*DVC* page 249).

THE TRUTH BEHIND THE CODE:

As already noted, the ∨ was not used as the female symbol (see this book, page 47). This sign is not even called a "chalice." It would more accurately be termed a type of chevron. "Chalice" is actually a Middle English word (derived from the Old French form of the Latin *calix* or *calic*). It simply means "cup." The word was not used to refer to any ancient symbol for a female or a womb.

The Priory of Sion

THE DA VINCI CODE:

The nature of the Priory of Sion. Currently headquartered in France, this organization is "one of the oldest surviving secret societies on earth" (*DVC* page 113).

THE TRUTH BEHIND THE CODE:

There have been at least three organizations called "The Priory of Sion." The first was a Roman Catholic monastic order founded in Jerusalem at the monastery of Our Lady of Mt. Zion in about 1100. This group of monks, known as the *Ordre de Notre Dame de Sion* (Order of Our Lady of Zion), ceased to exist in 1617, when it was absorbed by the Jesuits.

The history of the second and third Priories of Sion can be traced to the Frenchman Pierre Plantard (1920–2000), who in 1942 founded an anti-Masonic and anti-Jewish group known as Alpha

Galates.[19] Its periodical, *Vaincre* ("conquer"), was a mixture of anti-Jewish and anti-Masonic railings, pro-Nazi remarks, esoteric spirituality, and mythology.[20]

Little more is known about Plantard until 1953, when he received a six-month prison term for fraud and embezzlement.[21] Then, in 1956, he and three friends formed a social club "devoted to the cause of Low-Cost Housing."[22] They called their group the Priory of Sion and created a journal titled *C.I.R.C.U.I.T.*[23] This Priory dissolved within a year.

The third Priory of Sion, also started by Plantard, can be traced to the early 1960s, when he became obsessed with the idea of being an occult master and a descendant of kings. He recruited several followers and began a crusade to bring back the French monarchy via popularization of the notion that there existed a hidden royal bloodline in France. Plantard and his associates sought to achieve their goals by depositing forged papers in libraries, including the Bibliothèque Nationale (National Library) in Paris (see page 52).[24]

THE DA VINCI CODE:

Jesus and the Priory of Sion. The Priory learned of "a stash of hidden documents" that not only told the true story of Jesus and Magdalene, but also traced their holy bloodline (*DVC* page 158).

THE TRUTH BEHIND THE CODE:

This reference to "hidden documents" stems from a popular myth surrounding the French town of Rennes-le-Château and a priest named Saunière. Here is a brief outline of this tale:

Bérenger Saunière (1852–1917) became the parish priest of Rennes-le-Château in 1885. For years nothing about his life was out of the ordinary. Then, in 1891, he discovered four parchments (possibly five). Two were genealogies: the first dated 1244, which confirmed that the Merovingian bloodline had survived; and the second dated 1644, which was a continuation of the bloodline from 1244. The third parchment was a 1695 "Testament" penned by a François-Pierre d'Hautpoul, who at that time was the feudal lord of Rennes-le-Château. The fourth document, on its front and back, contained what looked like Latin portions of the Gospels.[25] But upon closer examination this latter document contained not just Gospel excerpts, but a complex sequence of codes embedded into the words taken from Matthew, Mark, Luke, and John.[26] One code read, "TO DAGOBERT II, KING, AND TO SION BELONGS THIS TREASURE AND HE IS THERE DEAD."

After showing the find to his superior, the Bishop of Carcassonne, Saunière was dispatched to Paris to show the parchments to "certain important ecclesiastical authorities."[27] No one knows what was said during these meetings, but after several weeks, Saunière returned to his church. He immediately began doing some very strange things: for example, erasing messages on tombstones, going on long journeys to collect rocks, writing letters to persons in France, Germany, Switzerland, and other countries.[28] Most curious, however, was his sudden wealth by 1917.[29]

Saunière then suffered a suspicious "stroke." A neighboring priest (Abbé Rivière) was called to hear Saunière's final confession, which he did in private. But when Rivière emerged from his encounter with Saunière, he was "visibly shaken." One witness said he "never smiled again."[30] Another said this poor priest "lapsed into acute depression" for several months.[31] Oddly, Saunière's will said that he was penniless.

This is the saga that inspired the book *Holy Blood, Holy Grail*—the primary volume Dan Brown used to concoct his thriller. (In fact, the author used the priest's last name for one of his characters: Jacques *Saunière*, the art curator whose murder opens the *Code*.) The truth, however, is that during Saunière's life nothing remarkable or mysterious happened—only something sordid. The priest acquired wealth, but not through buried treasure or parchments. He sold masses. In other words, he accepted money to say masses for devout Roman Catholics.[32] By the time his bishopric realized what was going on, Saunière had amassed a small fortune. But this led to his being "suspended from priestly duties in 1911" until his death.[33]

The Story Begins

How did the Saunière saga originate? The initial storyteller was a businessman, Noël Corbu, who purchased Saunière's estate and turned its guest house into a hotel. Corbu began spreading the tale in the mid-1950s because he had "opened a restaurant in the Villa Béthanie and needed a publicity gimmick to attract customers."[34] Two versions of Corbu's story exist: a transcript of a recorded message he made for guests in about 1956, and a publicity statement from about 1955. The versions are nearly the same, but contain many variants.[35]

The first published account of this tale appeared in a 1956 article entitled (in English translation) "The Priest's Fabulous Discovery of the Billions of Rennes-le-Château," which claimed "that Saunière had discovered a treasure—using Noël Corbu as his source."[36] Within a year, treasure hunters and religious pilgrims were in Rennes-le-Château, but nothing was found. (But this came as no surprise to many locals who had known Saunière.)[37]

Recent excavations of the property have continued to yield no confirmations of the Saunière myth. And yet it lives on, thanks to books like *Holy Blood, Holy Grail*, and its sequel, *The Messianic Legacy*. These volumes advance the theory that Saunière may have been paid off to keep silent about something he found—namely, the parchments that allegedly detail the lineage of Christ and Mary Magdalene through the Merovingian king Dagobert II.

THE DA VINCI CODE:

The documentation preserved. The hidden documents that detail the truth about Mary Magdalene, Jesus, and their lineage were long ago entrusted to the Priory of Sion (*DVC* page 160).

THE TRUTH BEHIND THE CODE:

As already noted, the contemporary Priory of Sion was founded by Pierre Plantard in the early 1960s. His link to "hidden documents" and the Bérenger Saunière saga goes back to the late 1950s or early 1960s, when he actually met the businessman Noël Corbu (see above): "[L]etters written by the two men to each other exist—as well as photographs of them standing together by the Tour Magdala in Rennes-le-Château. Pierre Plantard developed an interest in Corbu's story about Bérenger Saunière and decided to embellish it."[38]

In hopes of spreading his embellishments, which he believed would further his French monarchy–related political goals (see page 49), Plantard decided to begin planting numerous forged documents throughout France.[39] For example one paper, from January 18, 1964, was titled *Généalogie des rois mérovingiens* ("a genealogy of the Merovingian kings").[40] Although signed by a "genealogist" named "Henri Lobineau" and dated "1954," it was really authored by Plantard and his associates. This text includes several claims now embedded in the conspiracy theory of *The Da Vinci Code:* for example, that the Priory of Sion was founded by Godfrey of Bouillon and that the Merovingian line survived via King Dagobert II. Another false document (from August 1965) was *Les descendants Mérovingiens ou l'enigme du Razes Wisigoth* ("the Merovingian descendants, or the enigma of the Visigothic Razes").[41] It said that Saunière had found hidden parchments containing ancient knowledge.

A third forgery was *Les Dossiers Secrets d'Henri Lobineau* ("the secret records of Henri Lobineau," from about 1967). It contained an alleged list of Grand Masters of the Priory of Sion, including Leonardo da Vinci. This is the same text Dan Brown refers to in *The Da Vinci Code.* But he fails to note that 1) it was a false report created in 1967 by Plantard and his associates, and 2) its full title includes the pseudonym "Henri Lobineau." Brown just calls it *Les Dossiers Secrets.*[42]

A Primary Reference

As it turns out, Plantard was a main source of information for the authors of *The Da Vinci Code*'s primary reference work—*Holy Blood, Holy Grail.*[43] The popularity of *Holy Blood, Holy Grail* led directly to Plantard's conspiracy notion being picked up by what has become a host of propagators, including Dan Brown. But these recent advocates of the "bloodline" conspiracy seem unaware of a very possible source of Plantard's ideas—the far-right esotericist Julius Evola (1898–1974), an Italian fascist who imbued his political views with Celtic mythology, Holy Grail legends, and the rabidly anti-Jewish conspiracies of the anonymous work *Protocols of the Elders of Zion.*[44]

Author Robert Richardson has observed that "many 'Priory' themes originated with Evola's ideas."[45] Such an assertion is plausible. Plantard, it must be remembered, was anti-Jewish. During the Nazi occupation of France he clearly supported the German-controlled

Vichy government (early 1940s) and castigated Jews through his pub-lication, *Vaincre*. At the very least, he would have appreciated the speeches and writings of Evola, whose work was admired by many Nazi leaders, including Heinrich Himmler.

Evola, who held the old-world belief that kings were divine, saw state institutions as having a kind of sacredness. Evola also spoke of the "special quality of the blood which he alleged once existed in one royal house."[46] He even gave recognition to God-frey of Bouillon as "the ideal ruler, the *lux monarchorum* ('light of monarchs')."[47] According to Evola, "man could only be restored 'by a government of a spiritual elite,'" whose spirituality was to be marked by a belt, or cord, of initiation. Coincidentally, Plantard's Priory documents called for each member to wear "a cord at initi-ation."[48] Plantard may have taken Evola's views and blended them with the Saunière tale and yet other occult teachings.[49]

It should be noted, though, that Evola's ideas were not unique during the Nazi era, which means that Plantard's views may have developed independently of Evola. A more obvious influence on him was Paul Le Cour (died 1954), whose teachings were similar to those of the New Age. Le Cour blended esoteric spirituality with various apocalyptic elements of Christianity—for example, he preached that the coming Age of Aquarius would be marked by Christ's triumphant second coming. He also advocated formation of a knighthood and promoted legends of Atlantis. "Plantard did not so much 'copy' the ideas of Paul Le Cour but rather used them as a basis for his own creations of the 1960s and 1970s as found in the later Priory Documents relating to [the] Priory of Sion."[50]

Examining Plantard's sources exposes only the tip of an aston-ishingly massive iceberg that further involves historical discrepan-cies, unanswered questions, forged parchments, a plethora of pseudonyms, and false addresses. Yet Plantard's Priory continues to thrive, apparently under the leadership of his son, Thomas. And his myths continue to be spread through books like *The Da Vinci Code*.[51]

The Story Changes

What was the outcome of Plantard's career? Thanks to *Holy Blood, Holy Grail*, he enjoyed increased publicity and popularity for many years. In 1989 and 1990 he even revived his magazine *Vaincre*! Interestingly, its re-release just happened to coincide "with a new outbreak of anti-semitic crimes in France with accompanying anti-semitic literature."[52] It also was during this year that he totally restructured the Priory saga—something else not mentioned in *The Da Vinci Code*. For example, although the *Code* notes the year 1099 as the founding date of the Priory—the year given in *early* versions of Plantard's tale—Plantard himself contradicted this "fact."

In a 1989 *Vaincre* interview, he said that the Priory "was founded on 19 September 1738 in Rennes-le-Château by François d'Hautpoul and Jean-Paul de Nègre. If there are any connections pre-dating this then we are certainly not aware of them."[53] And with regard to Godfrey of Bouillon, Plantard suddenly began saying it was only his *spirit* that inspired others to found the Priory. He also changed the "secret" guarded by the Priory. It was now a "Black Rock" near the Château de Blanchefort that "contained an 'immense energy.'"[54]

Plantard's career, however, came to an ignoble end in 1993, when he found himself caught in the Pelat Affair—which involved the death of Roger-Patrice Pelat, formerly a close friend of French president François Mitterand. Pelat, "who was embroiled in a securities scandal and who consequently committed suicide,"[55] had been named by Plantard as a Grand Master of the Priory, which put him under suspicion. Plantard was then brought before the authorities, and after being questioned, he "admitted that he had made it all up."[56] After a search of his house yielded "a hoard of 'Priory Documents' that indicated that Plantard was the 'true King of France,' Judge Jean-Pierre Thierry concluded that Pierre Plantard was a harmless crank and issued him with a severe warning for 'playing games.'"[57]

THE DA VINCI CODE:

The founding of the Priory of Sion. The Priory was founded in Jerusalem in 1099 by the king of France, Godfrey of Bouillon, "immediately after he conquered the city" (*DVC* page 157). The Priory then "created a military arm—a group of nine knights...known as the Knights Templar" in order to retrieve the Magdalene documents "from within the ruins" of the temple (*DVC* page 158).

THE TRUTH BEHIND THE CODE:

This claim about the Priory's founding is taken directly from Pierre Plantard's spurious writings. The truth is, after King Godfrey conquered Jerusalem (about 1099), an abbey devoted to *Notre*

Image courtesy of Paul Smith, priory-of-sion.com

The 1956 official registration of Plantard's *Prieur de Sion,* or Priory of Sion. It includes the Priory seal, date of founding, and place of organization (Sous-Cassan, Annemasse, near the Swiss border). After Plantard reorganized the priory in the 1960s, his activities included spreading the Saunière myth not only by oral transmission, but through the use of false documents.

Dame de Sion (Our Lady of Zion) was established. Perhaps the earliest reference to knights being associated with it appears 600 years later, in the 1698 writings of a Father Vincent: "There were in Jerusalem during the Crusades...knights attached to the Abbey of Notre Dame de Sion who took the name of Chevaliers de l'Ordre de Notre Dame de Sion [Knights of the Order of Our Lady of Zion]."[58] But as their chosen name shows, the knights were devoted to the Virgin Mary, not Mary Magdalene.

THE DA VINCI CODE:

Proof from secret records. The Priory's existence was firmly established when documents found in the Bibliothèque Nationale (National Library) in Paris revealed the names of the Grand Masters of the Priory. These papers, which came to be known as *Les Dossiers Secrets* ("the secret records"), listed, among others, the Italian painter Botticelli, Sir Isaac Newton, the French author Victor Hugo, and Leonardo da Vinci (*DVC* pages 206, 326).

THE TRUTH BEHIND THE CODE:

This claim is based on Plantard's forged document *Les Dossiers Secrets d'Henri Lobineau,* which was planted in the National Library in 1967 (see pages 49, 52).

THE DA VINCI CODE:

French kings. The royal blood of Christ was passed down through the lineage of Dagobert II, the last Merovingian king (late 600s). The descendants of his son, Sigisbert, "included Godefroi de Bouillon—founder of the Priory of Sion" (*DVC* page 258).

THE TRUTH BEHIND THE CODE:

This is the same assertion made in *Holy Blood, Holy Grail.* Medievalist D.L. d'Avery (University College London, History Department) called this Merovingian–Godefroi theory "amiable lunacy." He added, "I have consulted a good specialist in the

Merovingian and Carolingian periods. She told me that she could find no evidence of the survival of the Merovingian line....[Y]ou would be on safe ground in assuming that the Merovingian line is of no historical importance after the eighth century."[59]

Interestingly, the whole theory of Christ's bloodline being continued through the Merovingians via Dagobert II relies on a very dubious event—the alleged marriage between Dagobert and a Giselle de Razès, daughter of the Count of Razes (*Razes* is the ancient name of the region of southern France that includes the town of Rennes-le-Château, formerly called *Rhedae*). The problem here is that "Giselle de Razès never existed. Plantard and his associates fabricated her."[60] The fabrication appeared in Plantard's forged *Généalogie des rois mérovingiens* (1964).

The Knights Templar

THE DA VINCI CODE:

The Origin of the Knights Templar. The order was founded by the Priory of Sion (*DVC* page 158).

THE TRUTH BEHIND THE CODE:

The Knights Templar were founded as a military religious order in about 1118, by Hugh des Payens, "a knight from Burgundy, and Godfrey of St.-Omer, a knight from N. France."[61]

THE DA VINCI CODE:

The Knights' true mission. It is a misconception that the Knights Templar were created to protect the Holy Land. Their public function of guarding pilgrims "was a *guise* under which the Templars ran their mission...to retrieve the documents [proving Jesus' bloodline and his relationship with Magdalene] from beneath the ruins of the temple" (*DVC* page 158).

THE TRUTH BEHIND THE CODE:

No historical evidence supports or even suggests this assertion.

THE DA VINCI CODE:

The location of treasure. One point on which "all academics" agree is that the Knights Templar "discovered something" beneath the ruins of the Temple and that this discovery "made them wealthy and powerful beyond anyone's wildest imagination" (*DVC* page 158). They took the treasure to Europe, "where their influence seemed to solidify overnight" (*DVC* page 159).

THE TRUTH BEHIND THE CODE:

First, it would be a difficult task to show that "all" academics agree that the Knights found something under the temple. Second, the Knights actually grew wealthy via gifts and donations from grateful pilgrims. There is no substantive documentation to bolster the *Code*'s claim. Third, it took many years (from about 1118 to 1290) for their influence and wealth to increase.

Moreover, the Knights actually became wealthy while still in Jerusalem—*before* leaving for Europe in 1291, the year all Christians were expelled from the Holy Land. Although they no longer had their crusading function, they continued to acquire wealth, which in turn made Europe's royal houses very uneasy. Particularly disturbed were those monarchs suffering from deficient funds, such as King Philip IV, who ruled a bankrupt France.

As for what *some* people think about the possible finding of a treasure by the Knights, guesses as to the nature of this treasure have ranged from the Ark of the Covenant to the Shroud of Turin. Other theories link the Knights to architectural knowledge or information that they sold for large sums of money, which in turn enabled medieval builders to construct the Gothic cathedrals that suddenly began to spring up all over Europe. (Many of these exhibited designs never seen before, "one of the first being Chartres which employed flying buttresses.")[62]

THE DA VINCI CODE:

The Knights' financial activities. The Knights Templar became so powerful that they were able to establish "modern

> banking" (*DVC* page 159). They actually "*invented* the concept of modern banking" (*DVC* page 346).

THE TRUTH BEHIND THE CODE:

The Knights Templar, like other knights, were simply involved in the financial and banking operations of Europe.[63] The concept of "modern" banking started in England during the seventeenth century. It represented an entirely new set of practices that replaced *traditional* "commodity form" banking with *modern* "debt form" banking.[64]

Nor were Knights associated with the invention of commodity banking. This form of banking dates back to ancient Mesopotamia "where the royal palaces and temples provided secure places for the safe-keeping of grain and other commodities."[65] Private citizens then became involved, which prompted the inclusion of banking rules in the Code of Hammurabi (1800 to 1700 B.C.). The Greeks refined banking, thereby enabling the Romans to effectively use it.

Here is where the *Code's* history seems to get confused. Banking, as it had existed, did fall into disuse after Rome's collapse (about 476). So "banking" had to be re-invented, so to speak. But the Knights Templar had nothing to do with resurrecting such practices. This occurred in France and in "Italian city states such as Rome, Venice and Genoa."[66] Central to it were *bills of renewal,* the first concrete evidence of which appears in Genoa in 1156.[67]

The Crusades helped stimulate banking because money and supplies needed to be rapidly transported over large distances. Consequently, "the Knights of the Temple and the Hospitallers began to provide some banking services such as those *already being developed* in some of the Italian city states."[68]

The false ideas in *The Da Vinci Code* may have come from a BBC Internet article on the Knights Templar. This article makes an assertion that is nearly identical to Dan Brown's: "The Templars devised the modern banking system."[69] Oddly, this same BBC information site, in an article about banking, clarifies the issue: "The *basic idea* of banking, and the typical services offered, can be traced back to *medieval times*."[70] The article then states quite clearly, "Modern banking originated in Europe in the 17th Century.[71]

THE DA VINCI CODE:

The destruction of the Knights. Pope Clement V "decided something had to be done" about the Knights Templar, so working in concert with France's King Philip IV, the Pope "issued secret sealed orders to be opened simultaneously by *his soldiers* all across Europe" on October 13, 1307. The "letter" said that all the Knights were to be rounded up and executed. "*On that day,* countless knights were captured" and killed, though some "managed to escape the Vatican purge" (*DVC* pages 159–160, emphasis added).

THE TRUTH BEHIND THE CODE:

Actually, it was King Philip IV who initiated a move against the Knights, hoping to acquire their land and money. He started his assault by gathering questionable witnesses, who testified that the Knights were involved in homosexuality, defiling the cross, and idol worship. Then Philip ordered *his* soldiers—not the Pope's—to make a mass arrest on October 13, 1307. This is the date on which the Knights were taken into custody, not executed, as the *Code* states. Afterward, Philip held a trial and found many of the Knights guilty, basing his verdict on confessions extracted by torture.

As for Clement's role, it has been noted by the Oxford-based medieval historian and Celtic scholar Karen Ralls that "the king did not proceed in the arrests of the Templars 'through letters of the Pope.'"[72] Ralls here is quoting from "The Trials of the Templars Revisited," written by the widely respected Malcolm Barber, professor of Medieval European History at the University of Reading in Berkshire, England.[73]

Historians agree that Clement was a terribly weak pope and was almost subservient to Philip. And yet, when he heard about what the French king had done, he not only annulled the entire trial, but also suspended the powers of the bishops involved and their inquisitors. Unfortunately, Philip had already released to the public his list of the crimes to which so many of the Knights had confessed, and the outrage of the masses now became a factor.

Then, in June 1308, Philip forced 72 Knights to publicly admit their crimes before the Pope himself. The testimony was so convincing that Clement himself began to wonder about the Knights.

So he opened a new commission to make an investigation of the charges. But this investigation and trial was still to be done on a local level throughout Europe. The *Code* conveniently fails to mention that at the trials in Portugal, Spain, Germany, Cyprus, and most of Italy, the Templars were found innocent and released.

In France, however—the seat of Philip's power—things went differently. Using a rather intricate interpretation of various laws on heresy, enemies of the Knights were able to secure the execution of 54 Templars. They were burned on May 12, 1310, not in 1307.

Then, under pressure from Philip and others, Clement decided in 1312 to dissolve the Order of the Knights Templar. This was actually a middle-of-the-road decision because Philip's supporters were demanding a full *condemnation* of the Order, while others were appealing for a *continuation* of the Order. Clement, rather than incur the wrath of either side, simply dissolved the Kinghts Templar, thus avoiding any official condemnation of the Order as a whole.

The *Code* also fails to note the story's ending. Those Knights who maintained that they were innocent were allowed to either join another military order or retire. In the latter case, they received a pension taken from the possessions of their defunct order. Many Knights actually chose the first option and joined the Order of Hospitallers, also known as the Knights of Rhodes. Sadly, there remained several Templars in custody whose statements had made it virtually impossible for them to be released. They were condemned and executed on March 16, 1314. In the end, about 120 Templars died.

❖ ❖ ❖

The numerous documents cited in this chapter have shown that Dan Brown's entire book depends on an "alternate history"— one based primarily on the scandalous, even criminal, actions of Pierre Plantard, founder of the modern Priory of Sion. Nonetheless, we are still left with the need to address the main contention of *The Da Vinci Code*—that Leonardo da Vinci not only was connected to the Priory, but actually embedded coded images into his art that relate to the supposed secret guarded by the Priory. Do these "codes" truly exist—and if so, do they reveal Leonardo's belief in a bloodline of Christ, the sacred feminine (or "the goddess"), and the corruption of the Church? Such pressing concerns will be dealt with in our final pages.

Chapter 5

Leonardo, the Mona Lisa, and *The Last Supper*

Truth at last cannot be hidden....Falsehood puts on a mask.
[But] Nothing is hidden under the sun. Fire is to represent
truth because it destroys all sophistry and lies; and
the mask is for lying and falsehood which conceal truth.

Leonardo da Vinci (1452–1519), artist, philosopher, scientist[1]

Leonardo da Vinci was a genius—brilliant, talented, and contemplative. He was also enigmatic, concealing his true self in cryptic notebook messages and subtle images in his art. Much has been written about Leonardo, yet only now are scholars beginning to understand the more puzzling aspects of his life. Sadly, some people who understand little about the man and his art have taken advantage of the mystique surrounding him. They recreate him into what they think he *should* have been—namely, one who shares their take on life. But as the artist himself said, "Truth at last cannot be hidden."

❖ ❖ ❖

Leonardo's Beliefs and Activities

THE DA VINCI CODE:

The artist and alchemy. Leonardo believed "he possessed the alchemic power to turn lead into gold and even cheat God by creating an elixir to postpone death" (*DVC* page 45).

THE TRUTH BEHIND THE CODE:

The great artist did *not* believe he had alchemic powers, nor did he claim to possess any elixir of life. He sometimes used the terminology of the alchemist in his writings (for example, references to Jupiter, Venus, or Mercury), but this was done in order to hide from his rivals the ingredients of materials he was using for projects.[2] He also used alchemic language to hide the procedures he had developed for making the metal alloys. For example, "describing a metal as having to be 'returned to its mother's breast'" meant that it "had to be returned to the fire."[3]

Specific references in Leonardo's notebooks to alchemy and alchemists are quite mocking. He loathed superstition, a category into which he heartily lumped necromancy (a practice "believed by small wits") and alchemy (the "sister" of necromancy). However, he did not view alchemy quite as negatively as necromancy, because at least alchemy produced substances like glass.[4] Nonetheless, he still had harsh words for this practice (see page 70), derisively calling alchemists "would-be creators of gold and silver."[5]

THE DA VINCI CODE:

A goddess-worshipper. Leonardo used "hidden symbolism that was anything but Christian" (*DVC* pages 45–46). He was a "well-documented devotee" of the ways of the goddess (*DVC* page 96).

THE TRUTH BEHIND THE CODE:

If Leonardo held any beliefs contrary to the Church, they had more to do with science than with any goddess. In the 1550 book *Lives of the Artists* by Giorgio Vasari, we learn that Leonardo "formed in his mind a doctrine so heretical that he depended no more on any religion, perhaps placing scientific knowledge higher than Christian faith."[6]

Such an observation indicates that the artist, for much of his life, probably was not a very good Roman Catholic. He was terribly offended by priests, who, he said, "produce many words, receive much wealth, and promise paradise."[7] He also saw "commercial exploitation" of Christians, who were duped into buying holy relics, such as the bones of martyred saints.[8] In other words, he despised the Church's religious trappings—but not necessarily the Church's declaration that there existed a Creator–God. He separated the two issues.

Based on his writings, the "God" that Leonardo embraced seems to have been a kind of glorification of the power, wonder, and beauty of nature. And yet he clearly attributed these glorious things to a single Creator, "whom he called *primo motore* ['prime mover']: the *inventor* of everything."[9] This Creator, of course, was far more abstract than the one preached by the Church. Near the end of his life, however, Leonardo apparently returned to the Church.

According to Vasari's biography, he desired "'to be informed of Catholic practice and of the good and holy Christian religion, then, after many tears, he repented and confessed.'"[10] Lest anyone think this is just a Christianity-exalting legend, Leonardo's will seems to affirm his return to religion. In this document, dictated before witnesses, the artist "commends his soul to Almighty God" (not the goddess), "to the Blessed Virgin Mary" (not Magdalene), and "to Saint Michael and all the angels and saints in paradise."[11]

THE DA VINCI CODE:

Involvement with the Priory of Sion. Leonardo "presided over the Priory between 1510 and 1519" (*DVC* page 113).

THE TRUTH BEHIND THE CODE:

This assertion is based on *Les Dossiers Secrets d'Henri Lobineau,* a document forged in 1967 by Pierre Plantard (see page 52).

Who Is Mona Lisa?

THE DA VINCI CODE:

The greatest work. Of the Mona Lisa, Leonardo claimed that it "was his finest accomplishment. He carried the painting with him whenever he traveled and, if asked why, would reply that he found it hard to part with his most sublime expression of female beauty" (*DVC* page 119).

THE TRUTH BEHIND THE CODE:

The artist worked on the Mona Lisa for at least four years, and perhaps as many as ten years, beginning around 1503 to 1506. He did not carry it around with him "whenever he traveled," nor did he tell people "he found it hard to part with." No one knows why it remained with him when he moved to France in 1516. There are many theories. Some say that whoever commissioned it grew tired of waiting and canceled the order. Others think that the woman whose portrait the Mona Lisa is, may have died. Leonardo himself, however, never gave an explanation.

THE DA VINCI CODE:

Man and woman blended. The Mona Lisa "is neither male nor female. It carries a subtle message of androgyny. It is a fusing of both"—and may actually have been a self-portrait of Leonardo as a woman! "[C]omputerized analysis of the Mona Lisa and da Vinci's self-portraits confirms some startling points of congruency in their faces" (*DVC* page 120).

THE TRUTH BEHIND THE CODE:

The woman pictured in the Mona Lisa is just that—a woman. Although her identity cannot be conclusively proved, she is thought to be Lisa Gherardini del Giocondo, the wife of Francesco del Giocondo. Other possible women named by art historians and scholars are Costanza d'Avalos, Isabella d'Este, and Giuliano de' Medici. In *Leonardo: The Artist and the Man*, biographer Serge Bramly remarks, "The most far-fetched theory is that this is a portrait of a man, or indeed a self-portrait by the artist."[12]

David Alan Brown, curator of Italian Renaissance painting at the National Gallery of Art in Washington, DC, concurs. In reference to the Mona Lisa, he notes that "'everything has been said about that painting'—that it is a self-portrait, a mistress portrait, a male lover, a woman who had breast cancer or who was bereaved or pregnant or both. 'I was amused by these things in the beginning,' Brown says. 'But now I find them tedious.'"[13]

As for the "startling points of congruency" between the face of Mona Lisa and the face of Leonardo in his "self-portraits" (plural, indicating several), these would be difficult to obtain since there only exists one uncontested self-portrait of the artist. It was sketched about 1512 and shows a grey-haired, long-bearded, 60-year-old man. X-rays of the Mona Lisa have revealed only that the original form of her face was, overall, "more oval and less spherical and the eye cavities were more deeply shaded. There is no trace of the smile in the x-ray...[and it] shows repeated reworking by the painter."[14]

THE DA VINCI CODE:

The name's ancient origin. The name *Mona Lisa* comes from the names of two Egyptian deities: the god *Amon,* and the goddess *Isis,* whose "ancient pictogram was once called L'ISA." *Mona Lisa* "is an anagram of the divine union of male and female" (*DVC* page 121).

THE TRUTH BEHIND THE CODE:

First, Leonardo himself did not even name this painting. He never titled *any* of his works. As far back as the "1525 inventory of the estate that the painter Salai, Leonardo's pupil and heir, left to his sisters," the painting is referred to only as "a portrait of a lady."[15] Just a few months before the artist's death in 1519, the cardinal of Aragon called it "the portrait from life of a Florentine lady." And the earliest royal inventories call it either "a courtesan in a gauze veil" or "a virtuous Italian lady."[16] The name we are familiar with did not appear until Giorgio Vasari's 1550 book *Lives of the Artists.* And this author is the only early source that calls it the *Monna Lisa*—which in English was shortened to *Mona Lisa.* Vasari originated the name.

Second, as we just noted, the actual spelling of the painting's appellation in Italian is *Monna* Lisa. *Monna* is a contraction of *madonna*—that is, *madame*. The name simply means *Madame Lisa*.

Hidden Messages and Painted Codes

THE DA VINCI CODE:

Secrets of the Madonna. Leonardo's true beliefs were reflected in the original *Madonna of the Rocks*, which was commissioned by nuns who asked him to paint "the Virgin Mary, baby John the Baptist, [the angel] Uriel, and baby Jesus sheltering in a cave." But "rather than the usual Jesus-blessing-John scenario, it was the baby John who was blessing Jesus...and Jesus was submitting to his authority." And Mary's hand was above the infant John "making a decidedly threatening gesture—her fingers looking like eagle's talons, gripping an invisible head." Finally, the angel Uriel is making "a cutting gesture" with his hand "[j]ust below Mary's curled fingers" as if "slicing the neck of the invisible head gripped by Mary." This original was later modified so that "everyone was arranged in a more orthodox manner." The second version is now in London's National Gallery under the name *Virgin of the Rocks*. But the original can still be seen in the Louvre. (All preceding quotes from *DVC* pages 138–139.)[17]

THE TRUTH BEHIND THE CODE:

Both versions of the painting are actually referred to as *Virgin of the Rocks*. The first one was painted in about 1483 to 1486, while the second one dates to about 1491 to 1495.[18] There is also an error about the commission of the work. The original 1483 contract with Leonardo asks for the Virgin to be pictured *with prophets*.[19] This is only the first of many such errors. Even the two babies are confused—with Jesus incorrectly identified as John.

The Da Vinci Code also does not take into account the fact that Leonardo was only one of several artists who were commissioned by the nuns for works of art. And as late as 1491, these artists were still bickering with the nuns over payment. They petitioned for more money that year, then entered into a legal battle with the confraternity over the value of their work[20]—finally calling for official arbitration, complete with experts, to judge the monetary value of the masterpieces.

Consequently, it is only a theory that *Virgin of the Rocks* was rejected by the nuns. Some art historians believe that the original 1486 painting was never even delivered. The 1491 petition suggests as much, as does the arbitration verdict of 1506. This ruling, which took into consideration all that had happened since 1483, makes no mention of a painting substitution or return (although other documents suggest that there *might* have been a rejection of the piece). The group of artists, Leonardo included, sold their *original* paintings (such as the 1486 *Virgin of the Rocks*) as the arbitration wore on, eventually to take 15 years. In fact, by 1491 they already had a buyer, which had prompted their petition for more money.

If the nuns did indeed reject the work, it was probably because Leonardo had changed it from the contractual terms, which were highly detailed. The work was supposed to have included two prophets. Mary was to have been dressed in gold, blue, and green. God the Father should have been floating overhead, while Jesus was to have been seated on a golden platform.

It is true that some elements in the original *Virgin of the Rocks* are quirky. It is also true, however, that no one really knows what they mean. Several guesses have been made, but we simply do not know what Leonardo was thinking. It might be a very personal painting by the artist, who often incorporated self-expression into his work: thoughts, feelings, memories, and beliefs. Or he may have been inspired by the Gnostic-influenced *Apocalypsis Nova* by the Franciscan theologian Amadeus of Portugal. In the absence of any documentation by Leonardo that further explains the painting, it is all a matter of guesswork.

Virgin of the Rocks is in many ways so strange that it "transports us into an unreal space and time, defying analysis."[21] The true meaning of its oddities, of course, might not go any deeper than Leonardo's irritation with the nuns, who made the mistake of telling him *exactly* what to paint. As ultimate freethinker and consummate artist, Leonardo might have simply used his brush to say, as it were, "You want details? Okay, fine. How do you like *these* details?" One can almost hear Gabriel in the original version making this statement. The angel is actually looking away from the scene, pointing a finger and practically smirking.

No one, it seems, will ever know the truth. But the one key thing forgotten in *The Da Vinci Code* is this: Leonardo was an *artist*—unbound by reality, obsessed with innovation. He never copied. He created. And with his creativity he saw the world, including its religious forms, differently. His art expressed his feelings. To caricature his artistry and creativity using unsupported, simplistic, goddess-centered assertions is an insult to both the man and his work.

THE DA VINCI CODE:

Leonardo's opinion of the New Testament. In his "notebook on polemics and speculation," Leonardo made the following comments about the Bible's New Testament: 1) "Many have made a trade of delusions and false miracles, deceiving the stupid multitude"; 2) "Blinding ignorance does mislead us. O! Wretched mortals, open your eyes" (*DVC* page 231).

THE TRUTH BEHIND THE CODE:

The first statement quoted in *The Da Vinci Code* is *not* about the Bible. Ironically, it is actually about *alchemists*. In full, Leonardo wrote, "The false interpreters of nature declare that quicksilver is the common seed of every metal, not remembering that nature varies the seed according to the variety of the things she desires to produce in the world. And *many have made a trade of delusions and false miracles, deceiving the stupid multitude.*"[22]

The second statement also is not about the Bible—nor is it even from the "notebook on polemics and speculation." It is from Leonardo's "Morals," a group of proverb-like sayings that relate to life in general: for example, study, food, love. Moreover, the artist's words have been altered in order to make them work for the *Code*. The actual statement by Leonardo reads,

> The greatest deception men suffer is from their own opinions. Folly is the shield of shame, as unreadiness is

that of poverty glorified. Blind ignorance misleads us thus and delights with the results of lascivious joys. Because it does not know the true light. Because it does not know what is the true light. Vain splendour takes from us the power of being—behold! for its vain splendour we go into the fire, thus blind ignorance does mislead us. That is, *blind ignorance so misleads us that...* [Leonardo deliberately stops his sentence for effect] *O! wretched mortals, open your eyes.*"[23]

THE DA VINCI CODE:

Seeing through the artist's eyes. Leonardo's painting *The Last Supper* contains several hidden signs that Mary Magdalene was the Holy Grail and that the apostle Peter hated her:

1. Magdalene is pictured to the right of Jesus. She has "flowing red hair, delicate folded hands, and the hint of a bosom....[It is] without a doubt...female" (*DVC* page 243).

2. Magdalene and Jesus are shown as a pair, "mirror images of one another"; and Jesus, wearing a "red robe and blue cloak," is the inverse of Magdalene, who is in a "blue robe and a red cloak" (*DVC* page 244).

3. The figures of Jesus and Magdalene make not only a ∨, but also a "flawlessly formed letter M" (*DVC* page 245).

4. Peter is "leaning menacingly" toward Magdalene and "slicing his blade-like hand across her neck" (*DVC* page 248).

5. The painting depicts a disembodied hand "wielding a *dagger*" (*DVC* page 248).

THE TRUTH BEHIND THE CODE:

Here, at last, we have what Dan Brown calls "the entire key to the Holy Grail mystery" (*DVC* page 236). But his understanding of *The Last Supper* is highly skewed. For instance, the figure next to Jesus—historically identified as the apostle John—is not "obviously" a woman. It could easily be a man, as evidenced by Brown's own observation about it having only a "hint" of a bosom—and even that is being generous. This is not to say that anyone is ever going to confuse John with Aragorn from The Lord of the Rings. John appears decidedly nonmasculine. Why?

According to Bruce Boucher—Curator of European Decorative Arts and Sculpture at the Art Institute of Chicago—John's appearance reflects the way Florentine artists traditionally depicted Jesus' favorite disciple: "St. John was invariably represented as a beautiful young man whose special affinity with Jesus was expressed by his being seated at Jesus' right."[24] *Slate* magazine bluntly pointed out, "If da Vinci thought John looked like a girly man, that's one thing. But a girlish-looking figure in a painting isn't proof that Mary was present at the Last Supper, let alone that Jesus and Mary were married."[25]

Image licensed from The Bridgeman Art Library

Leonardo's age-damaged painting *The Last Supper* (created 1494 to 1498) does not contain the elements described in *The Da Vinci Code*. For example, Jesus and the figure called "Mary" in the *Code* are not painted as mirror images. The masterpiece draws one's focus to Jesus, who alone is centralized. To his right, the alleged "Mary" is grouped just as the other disciples are grouped—within a triad.

Moreover, if the figure next to Christ is not John, then we need to know where the apostle really is. It is highly doubtful that Leonardo would have left John out of the picture since he is known as the "beloved" disciple and is considered the author of a Gospel.

Shapes and Images

The *Code* also fails to adequately support the claim that Jesus and "Mary" are mirror images of each other. The only proof is the color of their robes—which is hardly compelling. A more thoughtful look at the painting shows a far more dramatic aspect of the scene's composition than robe colors—namely, that Jesus is given a place of definitive spatial centrality.

And the figure of "Mary," contrary to mirroring that of Jesus, is segregated from Christ in a group with Peter and Judas. Rather than being as equally in focus as Jesus, "Mary" appears in a disciple-triad like all the others: Bartholomew–James the Lesser–Andrew; Philip–James the Greater–Thomas; and Matthew–Thaddeus–Simon.

It is true that Jesus and "Mary" form a ∨⁄, but as we have seen previously, the *Code's* interpretation of this shape is erroneous. For all we know, it might symbolize *veritas* (Latin, "truth"), or perhaps the chasm of sin that separates Christ from Judas (grouped with Brown's "Mary"). Or maybe it means nothing at all.

Image licensed from The Bridgeman Art Library

Contrary to *The Da Vinci Code* assertion, Jesus and the figure to his right (John, or "Mary") do not form a perfect letter "M." Tracing along the outline of their bodies produces a sideways lightning-bolt shape.

As for the "flawlessly formed letter M," it is hardly flawless. The "M" shape that could potentially have been created by the figures of Jesus and John, or "Mary," is destroyed by the presence of hands belonging to Philip and James the Greater (on Jesus' left side), and the bodies of Peter and Judas (on John's, or "Mary's," right side). The result is more of a lightning-bolt shape: ⌐∨⁄.

A Threat from Peter?

And what of Peter? He is *talking* to "Mary," not "slicing his blade-like hand across her neck." Like the others, Peter is reacting to Jesus' announcement that one of those present is going to betray him (Matthew 26:21). He is leaning over Judas and touching the figure to the right of Jesus on the shoulder while leaning in to speak, as if he is trying to communicate with John, or "Mary," without Judas hearing him. This accounts for the inclination of John's head toward Peter and down, as if he is listening closely to hear a whisper. And Peter's left hand is in fact positioned

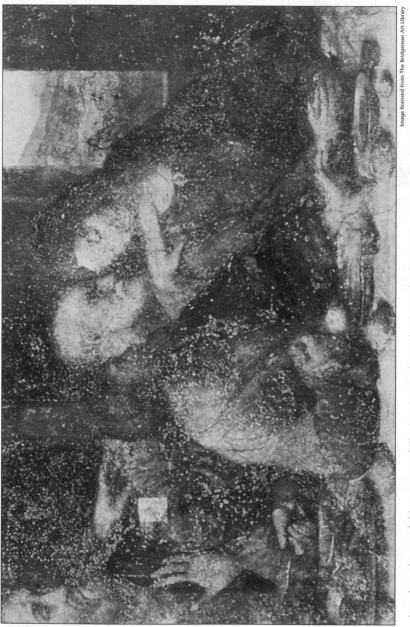

An enlarged copy of this segment of *The Last Supper* shows that it is indeed Peter's hand holding what *The Da Vinci Code* alleges is being held by a disembodied hand. Peter and John, or "Mary," are clearly talking in whispers to the side of Judas. Also, just in the frame, is the left hand of James the Lesser, which is positioned just like Peter's hand because he is trying to get Peter's attention.

Image licensed from The Bridgeman Art Library

similarly to the left hand of James the Lesser, who is trying to get Peter's attention by touching him on the back. Is James trying to "menacingly" slice at Peter?

Finally, there is the hand that is allegedly disembodied and dagger-wielding. In reality, it is Peter's right hand. Anyone can replicate his position by copying his movements. First, he rises from being seated, then turns left to speak with John. While doing so, he moves the knife he is holding downward, turning his arm counterclockwise, *away* from the direction he is moving, keeping his elbow flexed and wrist bent upside down.

This explanation of Peter's arm positioning is supported by a *Last Supper* study sketch that Leonardo made for Peter's right arm.[26] The sketch matches perfectly the arm in the painting, which is blue, the same color as Peter's robe. Comparing this drawing to *The Last Supper* clearly shows that the dagger in the painting is indeed being held by Peter. Art experts see it as a foreshadowing of the sword that Peter will draw in the Garden of Gethsemane in an attempt to defend Jesus. Its disembodied appearance is a result of faded line detail and dulling paint colors.

❖ ❖ ❖

Clearly, *The Da Vinci Code* has nothing to do with the real Leonardo da Vinci. Perhaps, in light of this, it would be best to conclude this chapter with the wise words of none other than the man who, if he were alive today, would no doubt raise a thundering protest against how his name and works have been misused. I, therefore, leave the reader with a message from Leonardo, taken from his "Morals":

> To lie is so vile, that even if it were in speaking well of godly things it would take off something from God's grace; and Truth is so excellent, that if it praises but small things they become noble. Beyond a doubt truth bears the same relation to falsehood as light to darkness....[T]he truth of things is the chief nutriment of superior intellects, though not of wandering wits.[27]

Facing the Facts

One's faith is an intensely emotional and highly sacred thing. Consequently, the religious views of all people must be shown respect and tolerance. This is not to say that everyone need agree on everything in order to get along, especially when it comes to complex issues like the Bible, Christ's identity, and the way of salvation. But it does mean we must strive to be as accurate as possible when discussing such topics.

Dan Brown's *The Da Vinci Code*, however, does the very opposite. It seems almost committed to misrepresenting a religious faith that hundreds of millions of people believe and hold dear.

This is not even a "Christian" issue. The issue is fact versus fiction. Truth versus lies. Accuracy versus inaccuracy. In other words, *The Da Vinci Code* would still be just as offensive if its misrepresentation of historical facts were used to attack Buddhism, Islam, or any other world religion instead of Christianity. This is because the most flagrant aspect of the *Code* is not that Dan Brown disagrees with Christianity, but that he utterly warps it in order to disagree with it—to the point of completely rewriting a vast number of historical events. And making the matter worse has been Brown's willingness to pass off his distortions as "facts" with which innumerable scholars and historians agree.

The truth is that Christianity is a religion solidly based on a variety of historical documents collectively known as the New Testament. These texts plainly tell the story of Jesus of Nazareth, a unique historical figure whose claims of divinity were accepted by a handful of followers, and eventually millions—people who changed the world. Although some individuals at certain periods in history have used Christianity for their own goals, the ever-present reality is that those who are faithful to the teachings of Christ have consistently shown the qualities that marked his life: love, compassion, gentleness, self-sacrifice, and integrity.

It also must be noted that Christianity is not anti-woman. In fact, it is one of the most pro-female religions in existence. The individuals who heralded the resurrection of Christ were women. Two of the Old Testament books are named after women (Ruth and Esther). And in the New Testament, Paul the apostle explicitly declared of those who are "in Christ" that "there is neither male nor female," but all are "one in Christ Jesus" (see Galatians 3:26-28). Further, throughout the Bible, numerous women are exalted as worthy of praise, honor, and reverence (for example, Deborah, Judges 4:4; Jesus' mother, Luke 1:26-56; Mary Magdalene, John 20:17-18; and Phoebe, Romans 16:1).

As for Dan Brown's fanciful conspiracy theory about the Church's cover-up of a Magdalene–Jesus union, it is almost beyond comprehension that a tale so rooted in demonstrable falsehoods could so quickly and easily be embraced by the public. Even more perplexing is how the whole Priory of Sion saga has been accepted by millions of people with equal alacrity. And yet *The Da Vinci Code*'s reputation as a factual book continues to spread. As of March 2004, countless Internet sites had been infected by dozens of quotes from the book—quotes that were being hailed as true statements.

But in the end, the truth will endure, and those who are willing to look at the facts will undoubtedly see it. Of this we can be certain. As the Old Testament tells us,

Truthful lips will be established forever,
but a lying tongue is only for a moment.

Proverbs 12:19

Notes

Thrilled by a Thriller

1. Stephen Rubin. Quoted in Bill Goldstein, "As A Novel Rises Quickly, Book Industry Takes Note," *New York Times*, April 21, 2003 (www.nytimes.com).
2. "Jesus, Mary, and Da Vinci," ABC Special, November 3, 2003.
3. Alyson Ward, "Decoding 'The Da Vinci Code,'" *Fort Worth Star-Telegram*, January 24, 2004, p. 1F (www.dfw.com/mld/dfw/entertainment/7800598.htm).
4. Charles Taylor, "'The Da Vinci Code' by Dan Brown," March 27, 2003, salon.com (archive.salon.com/books/review/2003/03/27/da_vinci/).
5. Taylor (archive.salon.com/books/review/2003/03/27/da_vinci/).
6. Dan Brown, *The Da Vinci Code* (New York: Doubleday, 2003), p. 248.
7. Brown, p. 249.
8. Brown, p. 233-234.
9. Brown, p. 257.
10. Brown, p. 257.
11. Brown, p. 257.
12. Brown, p. 257.
13. Brown, p. 254.
14. Brown, p. 158.
15. Brown, p. 159.
16. Brown, p. 257. However, a Roman Catholic tradition asserts that the bones of Magdalene have already been found. According to the Archdiocese of Milwaukee, "Charles, the nephew of King Louis XI, discovered Mary Magdalene's remains in 1279. Her remains were transferred to a crypt on May 5, 1280. Since 1295 the Dominicans have been guardians of her remains and the Basilica of Ste. Madeleine in St. Maximin [in France]. Her skull is displayed in the basilica and carried in procession on her feast day, which is a day of celebration in St. Maximin. Pilgrims and visitors fill the squares and streets of St. Maximin on July 22. On the eve of the celebrations, the golden reliquary

cradling the head of Mary Magdalene is removed from behind the grille over the tomb in the crypt and placed in yet a larger reliquary sculptured as a bust. It takes 12 men to carry the reliquary through the streets to the Monastery of Saint Mary Magdalene, home of the cloistered Dominicans" (www.archmil.org/news/ShowArchivedNews .asp?ID=1412).

17. Brown, p. 258.

18. Brown, p. 235.

19. Dan Brown. Quoted in "Explosive New Thriller Explores Secrets of the Church," no date, interview with Ed Morris, www.bookpage.com/ 0304bp/dan_brown.html.

20. Bob Minzesheimer, "'Code' Deciphers Interest In Religious History," *USA Today,* December 11, 2003.

21. Valerie MacEwen, "Try Putting This Book Down," www.popmatters .com/books/reviews/d/da-vinci-code.shtml.

22. "The Da Vinci Code: Book Review," *Counterculture,* counterculture .co.uk/book-review/the-da-vinci-code.html.

23. Taylor (archive.salon.com/books/review/2003/03/27/da_vinci/).

24. Brown, p. 1.

25. Dan Brown, interview with Borders, no date, www.bordersstores.com/ features/feature.jsp?file=browndan.

26. MM_NYC, January 25, 2004, Internet posting, www.cultofdanbrown .com/ubbthreads/showflat.php/Cat/0/Number/502/page/0/view/ collapsed/sb/5/o/all/fpart/1.

27. FTLouie34, December 19, 2003, Internet posting, www.cultofdanbrown .com/ubbthreads/showflat.php/Cat/0/Number/502/page/0/view/ collapsed/sb/5/o/all/fpart/1.

28. Richard Fox. Quoted in Linda Kulman and Jay Tolson (with Katy Kelly), "Jesus in America," *U.S. News and World Report,* December 16, 2003 (www.usnews.com [archives]).

29. Latin, "Untangle the subject and the truth will be evident."

Chapter 1—Conspiracy Theories, Mass Confusion, and Rewriting History

1. Sandra Miesel, "Dismantling The Da Vinci Code," September 1, 2003, *Crisis* magazine (www.crisismagazine.com/september2003/feature1.htm).

2. Dan Brown, *The Da Vinci Code* (New York: Doubleday, 2003), p. 21.

3. "The Louvre's Pyramid celebrates its 10th Anniversary From 7 to 21 April 1999," official Louvre Internet site, www.louvre.or.jp/louvre/ presse/en/activites/archives/anniv.htm.

4. Brown, p. 36.

5. Here are thumbnail sketches of Brown's plots: *Digital Fortress* (2000)— Reveals a conspiracy linked to the secretive National Security Agency. *Angels & Demons* (2001)—Exposes a conspiracy involving the infamous

Illuminati. *Deception Point* (2002)—Outlines NASA's role in a government conspiracy.

6. Dan Brown, "FAQ About Dan Brown," www.danbrown.com/novels/davinci_code/faqs.html.

7. Brown, "FAQ."

8. Kerr Cuhulain, *Full Contact Magick: A Book of Shadows for the Wiccan Warrior* (St. Paul, MN: Llewellyn Publications, 2002), p. 239.

9. Doreen Valiente, *An ABC of Witchcraft Past & Present* (New York: St. Martin's Press, 1973), p. 306.

10. In ancient Egypt, for example, it symbolized "the underworld or the kingdom of death" (see Carl G. Liungman, *Symbols '98 Encyclopedia*, online version of *Thought Signs: The Semiotics of Symbols—Western Ideograms* [Amsterdam: OS Press, Inc., 1994]), symbols.com/encyclopedia/30/3059.html.

11. John Michael Greer, *The New Encyclopedia of the Occult* (St. Paul, MN: Llewellyn Publications, 2003), p. 367.

12. Raven Grimassi, *Encyclopedia of Wicca & Witchcraft* (St. Paul, MN: Llewellyn Publications, 2000), p. 285.

13. Cuhulain, p. 103.

14. "Torch Run, Olympic Rings Not So Ancient," *The Herald-Mail*, July 14, 1996 (www.herald-mail.com/news/1996/olympics/july14herald.html).

15. "Torch Run, Olympic Rings." This article explains that the myth of the ancient origin of the rings "began with Leni Riefenstahl, the German cinematographer who chronicled Hitler's rise to power in the documentary 'Triumph of the Will' and extolled the 1936 Games in the 12-hour film 'Olympia.'...Riefenstahl had the rings carved into a rock at Delphi, Greece, as a backdrop for torch bearers circling the ruins of the ancient stadium. 'Years later, American authors Lynn and Gray Poole observed the old movie prop, mistook it for an ancient inscription, and published their error, which soon spread to other books, where it continues to mislead the unwary.'....The 'altar at Delphi' depicted in the Pooles' 1963 book, *History of the Modern Olympics*, eventually was moved from the stadium, but the myth persisted—even in the Official 1980 Olympics Guide, whose author, Gen. John V. Grombach, wrote: 'The interlocking circles found on the altar at Delphi are considered by experts to be 3,000 years old.'"

16. Grand Lodge of British Columbia and Yukon Web site, "Venus and the Pentagram," freemasonry.bcy.ca/anti-masonry/venus.html.

17. Lewis Spence, *The Encyclopedia of the Occult* (London: Bracken Books, 1994), pp. 402-403.

18. Charles S. Clifton, "The Unexamined Tarot," *Gnosis* (Winter 1991), no. 18, pp. 48-49.

NOTES

19. Ronald Decker, Thierry Depaulis, and Michael Dummett, *A Wicked Pack of Cards: The Origin of the Occult Tarot* (New York: St. Martin's Press, 1996), p. ix. Cited in Grimassi, p. 359.

20. Clifton, p. 44. Perhaps the most accurate theory is that the two halves of the tarot—i.e., the *Major Arcana* (22 picture cards) and the *Minor Arcana* (56 cards)—were created independently and blended to create the tarot we know today. It is theorized that the Major Arcana probably took shape in Europe, while the Minor Arcana originated within the Muslim kingdoms of Egypt and northern India.

21. Clifton, pp. 46-47.

22. Valiente, p. 354.

23. Thomas Banyacya. Quoted in *Christopher McLeod, Hopi Journal* (c. 1995), www.sacredland.org/ar1995.html.

24. Scott Peterson, *Native American Prophecies* (St. Paul, MN: Paragon House, 1990), p. 160.

25. Peterson, pp. 159-162.

26. Pagan worship was actually outlawed by Emperor Theodosius in 391. The confusion may stem from the 325 Council of Nicaea, presided over by Constantine. That council produced the first formal written expression of the Christian faith—the Nicene Creed. This same creed was used at the 381 Council of Constantinople to declare Christianity the state religion. Brown apparently confused these events and ended up thinking that Constantine made Christianity the state religion in 325.

27. At least one pagan intellectual, Galen, went so far as to write a favorable report about Christians. In his report about Christians, Galen discussed how he personally witnessed them "teaching and preaching a morality and way of life corresponding to that of philosophers" (Everett Ferguson, *Backgrounds of Early Christianity* [Grand Rapids: Eerdmans, 1987; 1993], p. 564).

28. F.F. Bruce, *The Spreading Flame* (Grand Rapids: Eerdmans, 1958; 1995 reprint), pp. 185-186. Christians also suffered persecution during the reigns of Nero (A.D. 54–68), Domitian (81–96), Trajan (98–117), Hadrian (117–138), Antoninus Pius (138–161), Marcus Aurelius (161–180), Maximinus (235–238), Gallus (251–253), and Valerian (253–260).

29. H.L. Ellison, "Sunday," in J.D. Douglas, gen. ed., *The New International Dictionary of the Christian Church* (Grand Rapids: Zondervan, 1974; 1978 rev. ed.), p. 940.

30. Ignatius said that Christians held a "new hope, no longer observing the Sabbath, but living in the observance of the Lord's Day." He further encouraged believers to "keep the Lord's Day as a festival, the resurrection-day, the queen and chief of all the days" (Ignatius, *The Epistle of Ignatius to the Magnesians* [long version], reprinted in Alexander

Roberts and James Donaldson, eds., *The Ante-Nicene Fathers* [Grand Rapids: Eerdmans, 1993], vol. 1, pp. 62-63).

31. Ellison, in Douglas, p. 940.

32. Philip Schaff, *History of the Christian Church* (Grand Rapids: Eerdmans, 1950 ed.), vol. 3, p. 105.

33. In other words, *Jehovah* is a mistransliteration, compounded by the fact that, while "J" has a "Y" sound in Latin, it has a very different sound in English—as in the word *jam*. *Jehovah* appears in no literature earlier than about the thirteenth century, and it began to be popularized in the sixteenth century by well-meaning but mistaken Christians.

Chapter 2—Gnosticism, Ancient Gospels, and the Bible

1. Quoted in Roxanne Roberts, "The Mysteries of Mary Magdalene: 'The Da Vinci Code' Resurrects a Debate of Biblical Proportions," *Washington Post,* July 20, 2003, D1 (www.danbrown.com/media/magdalene .html).

2. Hans Jonas, *The Gnostic Religion* (Boston: Beacon, 1963), p. 44.

3. Other Gnostics held that Jesus was indeed a man, but he was separate from "the Christ" (i.e., God's spiritual agency). In this version of Gnosticism, "the Christ" came upon Jesus at his baptism and left him at the crucifixion.

4. Ronald H. Nash, *The Gospel and the Greeks* (Richardson, TX: Probe Ministries, 1992), pp. 218,222.

5. See Elaine Pagels, *The Gnostic Gospels* (New York: Vintage Books, 1979; 1989 ed.), p. xviii; and Keith Hopkins, *A World Full of Gods* (New York: Plume, 1999), pp. 1,77,84. The conversion took place in 312 after the emperor had a vision, and then a dream, in which he saw "a cross of light." His experience occurred while on the battlefield facing Maxentius, who "was relying on pagan magic." So Constantine prayed. Then came his dream or vision of a cross. It supposedly bore the phrase "Conquer by this." Constantine obeyed, ordering his soldiers to fight under the banner of a cross inscribed with letters for the name of Christ. He was indeed victorious, which moved him to become a Christian (Kenneth Scott Latourette, *A History of Christianity* [Peabody, MA: Prince Press, 1997; orig. pub. in 1953 by Harper-Collins], vol. 1, pp. 91-92).

6. Philip Schaff, *History of the Christian Church* (Grand Rapids: Eerdmans, 1950 ed.), vol. 3, p. 30; cf. F.F. Bruce, *The Spreading Flame* (Grand Rapids: Eerdmans, 1958; 1995 reprint), p. 294.

7. D.F. Wright, "Constantine the Great," in J.D. Douglas, gen. ed., *The New International Dictionary of the Christian Church* (Grand Rapids: Zondervan, 1974; 1978 rev. ed.), p. 255. Constantine also freed Christian slaves, abolished customs offensive to Christians, contributed to

the building of churches, and gave his sons a Christian education (see Schaff, vol. 1, p. 31).

8. Wright, in Douglas, p. 255.

9. Bruce, p. 300.

10. Latourette, p. 93.

11. By A.D. 95, for instance, the Vatican Library contained the following books: Romans, 1 Corinthians, Hebrews, 1 Peter. By the late 100s, all of Paul's letters had been collected except for his writings to Timothy and Titus (Bruce, pp. 224-225).

12. Norman L. Geisler, *Baker Encyclopedia of Christian Apologetics* (Grand Rapids: Baker Books, 1999; 2000 ed.), pp. 529-530. Geisler gives the number of citations from the Gospels as follows: 268 by Justin Martyr (100–165), 1038 by Irenaeus (active in the late second century), 1017 by Clement of Alexandria (c.155–220), 9231 by Origen (c. 185–c. 254), 3822 by Tertullian (c. 160s–c. 220), 734 by Hippolytus (d. c. 236), and 3258 by Eusebius (c. 265–c. 339).

13. Bruce, p. 225. Bruce adds that there were certainly other gospels being circulated and that they enjoyed sporadic attention, but generally speaking, "the four gospels known to us were accepted to the exclusion of others from the early part of the second century."

14. Origen also mentioned four other works that were being debated, none of which were ultimately accepted: *Epistle of Barnabas, The Shepherd of Hermas, The Didache,* and the *Gospel According to the Hebrews.*

15. For example, Justin Martyr, Tatian, and Eusebius. The very first list of supposedly authoritative works came from Marcion (in about 140 to 150), who founded his own movement based on Gnosticism. He listed ten of Paul's epistles, as well as Luke's Gospel (although he deleted sections of it). Then, around 170 or 180, there appeared a list of 22 out of the 27 books now contained in the New Testament, including Luke and John (listed as the third and fourth Gospels). A copy of this list made in the seventh century is known as the Muratorian Fragment.

16. Milton Fisher, "The Canon of the New Testament," in Philip Wesley Comfort, ed., *The Origin of the Bible* (Wheaton, IL: Tyndale), 1992, pp. 73-74.

17. F.F. Bruce, *The Canon of Scripture* (Downers Grove: InterVarsity Press, 1988), p. 215.

18. Eusebius, *The Church History of Eusebius,* bk. 3, ch. 24, reprinted in Philip Schaff and Henry Wace, eds., *The Nicene and Post-Nicene Fathers* (Grand Rapids: Eerdmans, 1991), vol. 1, pp. 55-157.

19. The only major difference in today's Bibles exists between the Protestant Bible and the Roman Catholic Bible. The latter compilation of scripture adds several books to the Old Testament, including 1) Tobit; 2) Judith; 3) Book of Wisdom; 4) Ecclesiasticus (also known as The

Wisdom of Sirach); 5) 1 Maccabees; 6) 2 Maccabees; 7) Baruch; 8) Letter of Jeremiah; 9) Additions to Esther; 10) Prayer of Azariah; 11) Susanna; and 12) Bel and the Dragon. Although these books total twelve distinct works, they were added to the Roman Catholic Bible in a slightly different form. Numbers 1-6 were inserted as titled. Numbers 7 and 8 were combined into one book and inserted as Baruch. Number 9 was added at the end of Esther (already in the Old Testament). Numbers 11-12 were interspersed throughout the Book of Daniel (already in the Old Testament). The Jews, along with Protestants, do not accept these books as canonical.

20. F.F. Bruce, *The New Testament Documents: Are They Reliable?* (Grand Rapids: Eerdmans, 1977), p. 15.

21. It has been estimated, for example, that a comparison of New Testament documents would produce perhaps as little as one-half of 1 percent deviation in the text (Walter Martin, *Essential Christianity* [Ventura, CA: Regal Books, 1962; 1980 reprint], p. 19).

22. See A.K. Helmbold, "Nag Hammadi," in Geoffrey W. Bromiley, gen. ed., *The International Standard Bible Encyclopedia* (Grand Rapids: Eerdmans, 1986; 1990 ed.), vol. 3, p. 473. The dates offered in James M. Robinson's compilation of *The Nag Hammadi Library* (San Francisco: HarperSanFrancisco, 1978; 1990 ed.), pp. 38,124,141,524, are as follows: *Gospel of Truth* (c. 140–180); *Gospel of Thomas* (c. pre-200); *Gospel of Philip* (c. late 200s); *Gospel of Mary* ("sometime in the second century").

23. Only the *Gospel of Thomas,* according to a very limited number of scholars, even has the possibility of an earlier composition. Harvard professor Helmut Koester, for example, has suggested it "may include traditions even *older* than the gospels of the New Testament, 'possibly as early as the second half of the first century' (50–100)" (Pagels, p. xvii).

24. Irenaeus, *Against Heresies,* bk. 3, ch. 11, reprinted in Alexander Roberts and James Donaldson, eds., *The Ante-Nicene Fathers* (Grand Rapids: Eerdmans, 1993), vol. 1, p. 429.

25. Florentino Garcia Martinez, *The Dead Sea Scrolls Translated* (Grand Rapids: Eerdmans, 1992; 1994 Engl. ed.), pp. xxxvi-xxxvii. Brown seems to be referring to the first set of scrolls found at Qumran. These documents, however, are not the only "Dead Sea Scrolls." Moreover, they were not found in the 1950s. The *first* set of what would be *many* documents classed as the Dead Sea Scrolls was discovered in the Qumran area between late 1946 and early 1947. Similar texts that fall under the umbrella term "Dead Sea Scrolls" were discovered between 1951 and the early 1960s at various nearby locations. News of the discovery first appeared in a press release by the American School of Oriental Research in April 1948.

26. Martinez, p. 1. Martinez explains that they had their own *halakhah* (rules and guidelines for Jewish living), calendar, theological approaches, community structure, and view of the world—i.e., their practices forbade "contact with non-members."

27. Robinson, p. ix; cf. Pagels, pp. xxiv-xxvi.

28. For example, Ronald H. Nash (philosophy professor at Western Kentucky University); Francis Beckwith (Associate Professor of Church–State Studies, Baylor University); F.F. Bruce (Rylands Professor of Biblical Criticism and Exegesis at the University of Manchester in England).

29. See 2 Samuel 23:2; Isaiah 8:11; Jeremiah 30:4; Romans 3:2; 1 Corinthians 2:13; Hebrews 3:7; 10:15; 2 Peter 1:20-21; 3:15-16.

Chapter 3—Mary Magdalene, the Church, and Goddess Worship

1. Charles Taylor, "'The Da Vinci Code' by Dan Brown," March 27, 2003, salon.com (archive.salon.com/books/review/2003/03/27/da_vinci/).

2. Brown writes, "By fusing pagan symbols, dates, and rituals into the growing Christian tradition, he [Constantine] created a kind of hybrid religion....[P]agan religions in Christian symbology are undeniable....Nothing in Christianity is original" (*The Da Vinci Code*, p. 232).

3. John Michael Greer, *The New Encyclopedia of the Occult* (St. Paul, MN: Llewellyn Publications, 2003), p. 367. The mythic poem *Sir Gawain and the Green Knight* (about 1400) goes so far as to relate the points of the pentagram/pentacle not only to Christ's wounds, but also to the five knightly virtues (generosity, loving-kindness, self-control, courtesy, piety) and the five joys of the Virgin Mary (Annunciation, Nativity, Resurrection, Ascension, and Assumption).

4. Kerr Cuhulain, *Full Contact Magick: A Book of Shadows for the Wiccan Warrior* (St. Paul, MN: Llewellyn Publications, 2002), p. 241.

5. Greer, p. 199.

6. "[There were] hundreds or even thousands of them, forming a wildly diverse patchwork of belief and practice....No single generalization is true of them all. Some worshipped goddesses, while others did not; some were polytheistic, while others worshipped a single deity; and still others had objects of worship that are difficult to fit into the modern category of 'deity' at all" (Greer, p. 354).

7. Greer, p. 199.

8. Harrison argued "that prehistoric southeast Europe had been the site of an idyllic, peaceful, woman-centered civilization worshiping a three-fold goddess of nature. This civilization, she claimed, had been destroyed by patriarchal invaders before the dawn of history. These ideas were based on very little concrete evidence, and were fiercely

contested by other scholars. Despite this, they had an enormous impact on the popular imagination" (Greer, p. 200).

9. Greer, p. 200.

10. Greer, p. 200.

11. Greer, p. 200.

12. It is believed that Ramses III ruled 1184–1153 B.C. Other possible dates for his rule include 1180–1150 and 1182–1151.

13. P.L. Day, "Anat," in Karel van der Toorn, Bob Becking, and Pieter W. van der Horst, eds., *Dictionary of Demons and Deities in the Bible* (Grand Rapids: Eerdmans Publishing Co., 1999), p. 38; cf. A. Rowe, *The Four Canaanite Temples of Beth-Shan* (Philadelphia: University Museum, 1940), p. 33; H. Ringgren, John Sturdy, transl., *Religions of the Ancient Near East* (Philadelphia: Westminster Press, 1973), p. 142; and Rolan K. Harrison, "Queen of Heaven," *The International Standard Bible Encyclopedia* (Grand Rapids: Eerdmans Publishing Co., 1988), vol. 4, p. 8.

14. William J. Fulco, "Anat," in Mircea Eliade, ed., *The Encyclopedia of Religion* (New York: Macmillan Publishing Co., 1987; two-volume set), vol. 1, p. 262.

15. Day, in van der Toorn, et al., p. 37.

16. Fulco, in Eliade, vol. 1, p. 262.

17. The book, for example, condemned male magicians; male necromancers; and male wizards; men who become demon-possessed via their sinfulness; wicked men; and noblemen who harbor wizards. See *Malleus Maleficarum,* part 2, question 1, chapter 3 (www.malleus maleficarum.org/part_II/mm02a03a.html); part 2, question 1, chapter 16 (www.malleusmaleficarum.org/part_II/mm02a16a.html); part 2, question 1, chapter 10 (www.malleusmaleficarum.org/part_II/mm02a 10a.html); part 2, question 1, chapter 9 (www.malleusmaleficarum .org/part_II/mm02a09a.html); part 3, third head, question 34 (www.malleusmaleficarum.org/part_III/mm03_34a.html).

18. See "Medieval Medicine," www.intermaggie.com/med/women.php.

19. "The great majority of the men accused were poor peasants and artisans, a fairly representative sample of the ordinary population" (Robin Briggs, *Witches & Neighbours: The Social and Cultural Context of European Witchcraft* [New York: Viking Press, 1996]). Quoted in Adam Jones, "Case Study: The European Witch-Hunts, c. 1450–1750 and Witch-Hunts Today" (www.gendercide.org/case_witchhunts.html).

20. Brian A. Pavlac, "Ten Common Errors and Myths about the Witch Hunts," www.kings.edu/womens_history/witch/werror.html. (Pavlac is Director of the Center for Excellence in Learning and Teaching & Associate Professor of History, History Department, King's College.)

21. Carl E. Olson, "Cracking Up *The Da Vinci Code*," *Envoy Magazine*, August 23, 2003 (www.envoymagazine.com/envoyencore/Detail.asp? BlogID=1124).

22. Jones, www.gendercide.org/case_witchhunts.html.

23. Jones, www.gendercide.org/case_witchhunts.html.

24. Brian P. Levack, *The Witch-Hunt in Early Modern Europe* (New York: Longman, 1987), pp. 19-21.

25. Greer, p. 75.

26. Jones, www.gendercide.org/case_witchhunts.html.

27. Jones, www.gendercide.org/case_witchhunts.html.

28. Briggs. Quoted in Jones, www.gendercide.org/case_witchhunts.html.

29. Briggs. Quoted in Jones, www.gendercide.org/case_witchhunts.html.

30. Deborah Willis, *Malevolent Nurture: Witch-Hunting and Maternal Power in Early Modern England* (Ithaca, NY: Cornell University Press, 1995). Quoted in Jones, www.gendercide.org/case_witchhunts.html.

31. Willis. Quoted in Jones, www.gendercide.org/case_witchhunts.html.

32. Willis, p. 12. Quoted in Jones, http://www.gendercide.org/case_witch hunts.html; cf. Pavlac, www.kings.edu/womens_history/witch/werror .html.

33. Justin Martyr, *First Apology,* ch. 63, reprinted in Alexander Roberts and James Donaldson, eds., *The Ante-Nicene Fathers* (Grand Rapids: Eerdmans, 1993), vol. 1, p. 184; Justin Martyr, *Dialogue with Trypho,* ch. 36, reprinted in Roberts and Donaldson, vol. 1, p. 212.

34. Irenaeus, *Against Heresies,* bk. 1, ch. 10, reprinted in Roberts and Donaldson, vol. 1, p. 330.

35. Clement of Alexandria, *Exhortation to the Heathen,* ch. 10, reprinted in Roberts and Donaldson, eds., vol. 2, p. 202.

36. Irenaeus, *Against Heresies,* bk. 5, ch. 19, reprinted in Roberts and Donaldson, vol. 1, p. 547.

37. Craig Blomberg, "The Da Vinci Code," *Denver Seminary Journal* (2004), vol. 7 (www.denverseminary.edu/dj/articles2004/0200/0202.php).

38. Margaret Mitchell, as cited by Linda Kulman and Jay Tolson (with Katy Kelly), "Jesus in America," *U.S. News and World Report,* December 22, 2003 (www.usnews.com [archives]).

39. See comparison of texts in Karen L. King, *The Gospel of Mary of Magdala* (Santa Rosa, CA: Polebridge Press, 2003), pp. 16-17.

40. *Gospel of Mary,* pp. 17-19, reprinted in James M. Robinson, ed., *The Nag Hammadi Library* (San Francisco: HarperSanFrancisco, 1978; 1990 ed.), pp. 526-527.

41. Wesley W. Isenberg, "The Gospel of Philip," in Robinson, p. 139.

42. Isenberg, in Robinson, p. 140.

43. Richard Leigh, Internet site, www.egoetia.com/about.html.

44. Brown even mentions a fictitious BBC documentary in *The Da Vinci Code*—one that featured *Leigh Teabing* (p. 217).

45. Picknett and Prince also believe that Leonardo da Vinci created the famed Shroud of Turin—the holy relic considered by some to be the burial garment of Jesus (Lynn Picknett and Clive Prince, *The Turin Shroud: In Whose Image?* [New York: Harper Collins, 1994]. For a detailed critique of this book, see Daniel C. Scavone, "Book Review of *The Turin Shroud: In Whose Image?*," www.shroud.com/scavone.htm). They also hold that there is yet another major conspiracy involving extraterrestrials, the CIA, British intelligence, ancient Egyptians, and assorted world leaders (see Lynn Picknett and Clive Prince, *The Stargate Conspiracy* [New York: Berkley Publishing Group, 2001]).

46. "History of Paris," www.discoverfrance.net/France/Paris/Paris_history .shtml.

47. "The Franks," *The Catholic Encyclopedia* (New York: Robert Appleton Company, 1909; online edition, 2003), vol. 6 (www.newadvent.org/cathen/06238a.htm).

48. Guy Bedouelle, "Mary Magdalene—The Apostle of the Apostles and The Order of Preachers," *Dominican Ashram*, vol. 18, no. 4, 1999, pp. 157-171 (www.womenpriests.org/magdala/bedouell.htm).

Chapter 4—The Grail, the Priory of Sion, and the Knights Templar

Note: All quotations and information from the Web site priory-of-sion.com are used by the permission of Paul Smith.

1. Robert Richardson, "The Priory of Sion Hoax," *Gnosis: A Journal of the Western Inner Traditions* (Spring 1999), no. 51, p. 49.

2. Mark Pesce, "The Executable Dreamtime," in Richard Metzger, ed., *Book of Lies: The Disinformation Guide to Magick and the Occult* (New York: The Disinformation Company, Ltd., 2003), p. 29.

3. Chrétien de Troyes, *Perceval,* reprinted in Roger Sherman Loomis and Laura Hibbard Loomis, eds., *Medieval Romances* (New York: Modern Library, 1957), pp. 63-64.

4. See John Matthews, "Healing the Wounded King," *Gnosis: A Journal of the Western Inner Tradition* (Spring 1999), no. 51, pp. 17-22.

5. John Michael Greer, *The New Encyclopedia of the Occult* (St. Paul, MN: Llewellyn Publications, 2003), p. 207.

6. Other Arthurian tales include *The Quest of the Holy Grail* (late medieval era), *Sir Gawain and the Green Knight* (14th century), and Sir Thomas Malory's *Le Morte d'Arthur* (15th century).

7. Carl G. Liungman, *Symbols '98 Encyclopedia*, online version of *Thought Signs: The Semiotics of Symbols—Western Ideograms* (Amsterdam: OS Press, Inc., 1994), www.symbols.com/encyclopedia/41a/41a7.html.

8. Liungman, www.symbols.com/encyclopedia/41a/41a7.html.

9. Liungman, www.symbols.com/encyclopedia/22/226.html.

10. Liungman, www.symbols.com/encyclopedia/04/0424.html.

11. Liungman, www.symbols.com/encyclopedia/04/0433.html.

12. Liungman, www.symbols.com/encyclopedia/02/0219.html.

13. Liungman, www.symbols.com/encyclopedia/49/499.html.

14. Liungman, www.symbols.com/encyclopedia/52/524.html.

15. Liungman, www.symbols.com/encyclopedia/39/3932.html.

16. Liungman, www.symbols.com/encyclopedia/04/041.html.

17. Liungman, www.symbols.com/encyclopedia/04/041.html.

18. Liungman, www.symbols.com/encyclopedia/04/0434.html.

19. A February 13, 2004, letter from the Chief of Services, Archives and Museum Department of the Bureau of Associations (Police of Prefecture Paris), stated, "In our archive holdings we have a small file— reference Ga P7—on Pierre Plantard....[He] seems to have been a young oddball, identifying hypothetical 'Judaeo-Masonic' conspiracies at regular intervals and repeatedly offering his services to the authorities but without anyone taking the slightest notice of him" (Paul Smith, "Two Secret Service Reports about the Alpha Galates," priory-of-sion.com/psp/id84.html. The actual Secret Service reports can be accessed at this online site).

20. The group's statutes read, "The Order is rigorously closed to Jews and to any member who is recognised as belonging to a Judaeo-Masonic order" (Statutes of the Alpha-Galates, dated December 27, 1937, priory-of-sion.com/psp/id21.html). Plantard also supported Hitler, saying, "I want Hitler's Germany to know that every obstacle to our own plans does harm to him also, for it is the resistance put up by freemasonry that is undermining German might" (*Vaincre*, January 21, 1943, no. 5, p. 3, priory-of-sion.com/psp/id86.html).

21. Plantard was sentenced by the court of St. Julien-en-Genèvois, according to a letter written by the mayor of Annemasse in 1956 to the subprefect of St. Julien-en-Genèvois. "The Judicial Archives relating to Pierre Plantard's prison sentences of the 1950s are located in the Tribunal de Grand Instance de Thonon-les-Bains [21 rue Vallon, BP 524, 74203]—this is the information provided in August 1995 by Hélène Viallet, then the Directeur des Archives départementales de la Haute-Savoie, located in the town of Annecy" (Paul Smith, "Pierre Plantard's Judicial Archives and Criminal Convictions," priory-of-sion.com/psp/id30.html).

22. Paul Smith, "Priory of Sion Debunked," www.anzwers.org/free/pos debunking/.

23. C.I.R.C.U.I.T. is an acronym for *Chevalerie d'Institutions et Règles Catholiques d'Union Independante et Traditionaliste'* (Knighthood of Catholic Rules and Institutions of the Independent and Traditionalist

Union—see documents located at priory-of-sion.com/psp/pcc/circuit 1956.html). This journal described itself as the organ of the "Organisation for the Defence of the Rights and the Liberty of Low-Cost Homes." André Bonhomme (a.k.a. Stanis Bellas), a founding member of the Priory, explained all of this to the BBC in 1996; saying: "The Priory of Sion doesn't exist anymore....It was four friends who came together to have fun. We called ourselves the Priory of Sion because there was a mountain by the same name close by. I haven't seen Pierre Plantard in over 20 years and I don't know what he's up to but he always had a great imagination" (Paul Smith, "The Real Historical Origin of the Priory of Sion," priory-of-sion.com/psp/id43.html).

24. Paul Smith, "Priory Documents and Articles linked with Pierre Plantard, Thomas Plantard and Philippe de Chérisey," priory-of-sion.com/psp/id24.html.

25. Michael Baigent, Richard Leigh, and Henry Lincoln, *Holy Blood, Holy Grail* (New York: Delacorte Press, 1982; 2004 Delta paperback ed.), p. 32.

26. Baigent et al., p. 33.

27. Baigent et al., p. 34.

28. Baigent et al., p. 36.

29. Baigent et al., p. 36.

30. This rumor was laid to rest by a friend of the priest, Monsignor George Boyer, who in a 1967 French newspaper stated, "[T]hat dear old Abbé Rivière, the curé of Espéraza, who died in 1929, and who was the Dean of Coursan (where I got to know him well) never smiled again after the death of the Abbé Saunière, to whom he had administered extreme unction, is another puzzling statement, as I myself saw him roar with laughter" (Quoted in Paul Smith, "The Real Truth about Saunière's Last Rites," priory-of-sion.com/psp/id125.html).

31. Baigent et al., p. 38.

32. He even "advertised in religious magazines and journals like *Semaine Religieuse*, *La Croix*, *L'éclair*, *L'express du Midi*, *L'univers* and *Le Télégramme* and the money just poured in from all over" (Paul Smith, "Source of Saunière's Wealth—The Real Truth," priory-of-sion.com/psp/id62.html; cf. Jean-Jacques Bedu, "Autopsie d'un mythe" ("autopsy of a myth"), www.renneslechateau.com/librairie/bedu.htm.

33. Smith, "Source of Saunière's Wealth," priory-of-sion.com/psp/id62.html; cf. Paul Smith, "Rennes-le-Château and the Bérenger Saunière Affair Chronology," priory-of-sion.com/psp/id91.html. Copies of Saunière's notebooks wherein he lists the masses he sold and his correspondence with buyers are available for anyone to read.

34. Smith, "Rennes-le-Château and the Bérenger Saunière Affair Chronology," priory-of-sion.com/psp/id91.html.

35. A transcription of Corbu's recording can be found at www.rennesle chateau.com/anglais/corbu.htm. It not only does *not* contain religious references, but it also does not match the *Holy Blood, Holy Grail* version of Saunière's story. The publicity statement is only available in the October 2003 issue of *The Journal of the Rennes Alchemist* (issue #4), www.cerclealpheus.com/backissues.html. Neither version mentions Jesus, a bloodline, or the Knights. They simply tell the story of Saunière and buried treasure.

36. Albert Salamon, "La Fabuleuse Découverte du Curé aux Milliards de Rennes-le-Château," *La Dépêche de Midi,* January 12, 13, 14, 1956. Cited in Smith, "Rennes-le-Château and the Bérenger Saunière Affair Chronology," priory-of-sion.com/psp/id91.html, transl., "The Priest's Fabulous Discovery of the Billions of Rennes-le-Château."

37. Consider, for example, the words of a Monsieur Espeut: "[T]he Abbé Saunière never found any treasure....My family knew the Dénarnaud family. In 1925, when I was 14 years old, I used to go up regularly to Rennes-le-Château. I used to go and see Marie Dénarnaud [Saunière's maid]....In the library of the Tour Magdala, I read all the correspondence of the priest with his ecclesiastical lawyer at the time of his trial at the court of Rome. It was by collecting money for saying masses that the Abbé Saunière was able to construct his estate. He published small ads in the Catholic press throughout the world. I was able to read their texts, and I have seen thousands of replies.... [B]etween the ages of 15 and 20, I thoroughly searched the area within a 500-metre radius of the Villa and the Tour Magdala. I never found the slightest evidence of a hidden treasure. I am telling you this out of respect for the truth" (*Midi Libre,* Febuary 13, 1973. Quoted in René Descadeillas, *Mythologie du trésor de Rennes,* pp. 107-108 [1974], priory-of-sion.com/psp/id138.html; cf. Smith, "Rennes-le-Château and the Bérenger Saunière Affair Chronology," priory-of-sion.com/psp/id91.html).

38. Paul Smith, "Priory of Sion Parchments and Steven Mizrach," anzwers .org/free/parchments/.

39. A list of forged documents can be found online at priory-of-sion.com/ psp/id22.html.

40. This was the first Priory document to refer to Saunière.

41. Transl., "The Merovingian descendants, or the enigma of the Visigothic Razes."

42. Paul Smith, "Priory of Sion and Jean Cocteau," anzwers.org/free/posde bunking/cocteau.html. It is known that Plantard wrote this document because tests have shown that it was produced by the same printing machine known to have created a 1961 document by Plantard.

43. Paul Smith, "The Priory of Sion Files," www.pharo.com/secret_societies /priory_of_sion/articles/sops_01b_the_modern_history.asp.

44. This volume, since the early 1900s, has served as *the* standard reference book for anti-Semites.

45. Richardson, p. 54.

46. Richardson, p. 54.

47. Julius Evola, *Revolt Against the Modern World*. Cited in Richardson, p. 54.

48. Richardson, p. 54.

49. Consider a possible connection with an occultist named Johannes Stein (a German associate of the famous occultist and Theosophist Rudolf Steiner). In his 1928 book *The Ninth Century: World History in the Light of the Holy Grail*, Stein not only gave his version of the history and symbolism of the Holy Grail, but actually offered a "Grail Bloodline." One side of this so-called bloodline "extends into the royal house of France. Another extends down to Godfrey of Bouillon" (Richardson, p. 54). But Stein never meant this list to be taken as a *literal* bloodline. Plantard, however, if he did read the book, may have misunderstood Stein's intention, which was to simply show that certain events in the lives of the people he listed probably inspired events, characters, or both in the Holy Grail story: "Stein's intent is actually to illustrate how the positive spiritual forces represented in the Holy Grail are sometimes manifested in the lives and actions of people....He did not in any way state or imply that the Holy Grail was, or that it represented, a bloodline" (Richardson, p. 54).

50. Paul Smith, "Pierre Plantard and the Priory of Sion Chronology," smithpp0.tripod.com/psp/id22.html; cf. Paul Smith, "Pierre Plantard, 'Le Poulpe' and Paul Le Cour (real name, Paul Lecour)," priory-of-sion .com/psp/id72.html.

51. *The Da Vinci Code* adds to Plantard's views the Magdalene–Jesus spin found in Dan Brown's reference book *The Templar Revelation*. Oddly, Brown fails to mention that this book's authors portray Jesus and Magdalene not as spouses, but as sex partners who engaged in ritualistic intercourse *(hieros gamos)* that was "not necessarily a love match." (Lynn Picknett and Clive Prince, [New York: Touchstone, 1997], p. 260). Instead, they ravished each other in "sacred prostitution," which put them in touch with the Divine. Magdalene, according to Picknett and Prince, actually was a pagan priestess who initiated Jesus into the joys of orgasmic spirituality. Although Brown alludes to all of this in the *Code* (pp. 305-310), he is never explicit. But he does repeat, almost verbatim, several assertions from *The Templar Revelation* about the Priory, the Council of Nicaea, and goddess worship (see, for example, Picknett and Prince, pp. 257-264).

52. Paul Smith, "The Secret of The Priory of Sion," priory-of-sion.com/ psp/id136.html.

NOTES

53. Pierre Plantard, interview with Noël Pinot, April 1989, *Vaincre*, no. 1, pp. 5-6 (priory-of-sion.com/psp/id132.html).

54. Paul Smith, "The 1989 Plantard Comeback," priory-of-sion.com/psp/id60.html. Smith provides online links to copies of letters and other documents in French that contain this new Priory tale.

55. Paul Smith, "Priory of Sion Legal Battles, Two Examples—1953 and 1993," anzwers.org/free/posbattles/.

56. Smith, "Priory of Sion Legal Battles, anzwers.org/free/posbattles/. What is the current state of Plantard's Priory? That is the mystery. Might it not be possible that those persons who are most committed today to advancing the Priory's notions about an ongoing Merovingian lineage are in actuality the surviving members of Plantard's Priory? Interestingly, Henry Lincoln (coauthor of *Holy Blood, Holy Grail*) has recently been wavering on his previous statements regarding the Holy Grail and related issues such as the Priory of Sion. He was asked during a 2001 interview for his comments. "'In my old age, I've decided to stick to that which can be verified,' Lincoln groused when asked for an update on the secret society" ("The Jesus Conspiracy," *Carpe Noctem*, 2001, www.carpenoctem.tv/cons/jesus.html; cf. Jonathan Vankin and John Whalen, "Those Wacky Christ Kids!" in *The Seventy Greatest Conspiracies of All Time* (Sacramento, CA: Citadel Press, 2001), excerpt online at www.conspire.com/priory.html.

57. Paul Smith, "Pierre Plantard and The Priory of Sion Chronology," priory-of-sion.com/psp/id22.html. Interestingly, the fraudulent nature of Plantard and the priory of Sion is widely known in France. There it was "[g]enerally debunked" as far back as the mid-1980s (Paul Smith, "The Priory of Sion and Alice Kell [Grailromantic]," home.graffiti.net/prioryofsion/poslist.html). Countless Internet sites and numerous books (for example, *Mythologie du trésor de Rennes* ["mythology of the treasure of Rennes," 1974] by René Descadeillas; *Le Fabuleux Trésor de Rennes-Le-Château: Le Secret de L'abbé Saunière* ["the fabulous treasure of Rennes-le-Château: The Secret of Abbé Saunière," 1986] by Jacques Rivière; and *Autopsie d'une Mythe* ["autopsy of a myth," 1990] by Jean-Jacques Bedu) have exposed the Priory of Sion and its supporting works, such as *Holy Blood, Holy Grail,* as little more than a grand hoax. However, these important materials are all written in French, which has made them difficult for Americans to access. Consequently, books like *The Da Vinci Code* have been able to attract millions of American fans who are completely unaware of Pierre Plantard and his connection to the whole story.

58. Laura Knight-Jadczyk, "The Grail Quest and The Destiny of Man—Part V-g: The Priory of Sion," www.cassiopaea.org/cass/grail_5g.htm.

59. D.L. d'Avery, letter to P. Smith, November 5, 1982, priory-of-sion.com/psp/id112.html.

60. Richardson, p. 54.

61. Robert G. Clouse, "Templars," in J.D. Douglas, gen. ed., *The New International Dictionary of the Christian Church* (Grand Rapids: Zondervan, 1974; 1978 ed.), p. 956.

62. BBCi, "The Knights Templar," March 13, 2000, www.bbc.co.uk/dna/h2g2/A272558.

63. Clouse, in Douglas, p. 956.

64. Commodity banking, the only kind existing during the medieval era, "based its credibility on a commodity which was said to embody the value it represented (gold or silver)." But England's modern debt form of banking "rested on a promise for future transactions (redeem a banknote in gold, etc.)" (Samuel Knafo, "The Gold Standard and the Origins of the Modern International Monetary System," www.isanet.org/noarchive/knafo.html).

65. Roy Davies, "Origins of Money and of Banking," www.ex.ac.uk/~RDavies/arian/origins.html#invention; cf. Glyn Davies, *A History of Money from Ancient Times to the Present Day* (Cardiff: University of Wales Press), 2002.

66. Roy Davies, www.ex.ac.uk/~RDavies/arian/origins.html#invention.

67. Roy Davies, www.ex.ac.uk/~RDavies/arian/origins.html#invention. According to Davies, these bills were issues "to enable two brothers who had borrowed 115 Genoese pounds to reimburse the bank's agents in Constantinople by paying them 460 bezants one month after their arrival."

68. Roy Davies, www.ex.ac.uk/~RDavies/arian/origins.html#invention, emphasis added.

69. BBCi, www.bbc.co.uk/dna/h2g2/A272558.

70. BBCi, "Banking," August 25, 2000, www.bbc.co.uk/dna/h2g2/A416530, emphasis added.

71. BBCi, "Banking," www.bbc.co.uk/dna/h2g2/A416530.

72. Karen Ralls, *The Templars and the Grail* (Wheaton, IL: Theosophical Publishing House, 2003), p. 78.

73. See Malcolm Barber, "The Trial of the Templars Revisited," in H. Nicolson, ed., *The Military Orders: Welfare and Warfare* (Aldershot, England: Ashgate, 1998), p. 49.

Chapter 5—Leonardo, the Mona Lisa, and *The Last Supper*

1. Leonardo da Vinci, "The Artist's Materials," in Jean Paul Richter, transl., *The Notebooks of Leonardo da Vinci* (1888), the Project Gutenberg E-Book of *The Notebooks of Leonardo da Vinci* (www.gutenberg.net/etext04/8ldvc09.txt).

2. Leonardo da Vinci, "Varnish [Or Powder]," in Richter, www.gutenberg.net/etext04/8ldvc09.txt.

3. Serge Bramly, *Leonardo: The Artist and the Man* (New York: Penguin Books, 1988; 1991 transl. ed.), p. 387.

4. Leonardo da Vinci, "Polemics—Speculation," in Richter, www.guten berg.net/etext04/8ldvc09.txt.

5. Leonardo, "Polemics—Speculation," in Richter, www.gutenberg.net/ etext04/8ldvc09.txt.

6. Giorgio Vasari. Quoted in Bramly, p. 12.

7. Bramly, p. 274.

8. Bramly, p. 275

9. Bramly, p. 275.

10. Vasari. Quoted in Bramly, p. 406.

11. Vasari. Quoted in Bramly, p. 406.

12. Bramly, p. 363.

13. David Alan Brown. Quoted in "A Work in Progress," 2000, *This Day Online,* www.thisdayonline.com/archive/2003/01/12/20030112art03 .html.

14. Pietro C. Marani, *Leonardo da Vinci: The Complete Paintings* (New York: Harry N. Abrams, Inc., 1999; 2003 ed.), pp. 198-199.

15. Marani, p. 183.

16. See Bramly, p. 362.

17. This can be viewed and magnified for inspection at www.kfki.hu/ ~arthp/html/l/leonardo/02/2virg_p.html.

18. Marani, p. 138.

19. Marani, p. 130.

20. Marani, p. 136.

21. Bramly, p. 191.

22. Leonardo, "Polemics—Speculation," in Richter, www.gutenberg.net/ etext04/8ldvc09.txt, emphasis added.

23. Leonardo, "Morals," in Richter, www.gutenberg.net/etext04/8ldvc09 .txt, emphasis added.

24. Bruce Boucher, "Does 'The Da Vinci Code' Crack Leonardo?" *New York Times,* August 3, 2003, (www.nytimes.com [archives]).

25. Sian Gibby, "Mrs. God," November 3, 2003, *Slate* magazine (slate.msn .com/id/2090640).

26. Windsor Castle, Royal Library, inv. 12546. This sketch has been repro- duced in Marani, p. 231.

27. Leonardo, "Morals."